The Milford Series
Popular Writers of Today
ISSN 0163-2469
Volume Forty-One

GEORGE ORWELL'S GUIDE THROUGH HELL

A PSYCHOLOGICAL STUDY OF *1984*

by

Robert Plank

Edited by Robert Reginald

The Borgo Press
An Imprint of Wildside Press
Doylestown, Pennsylvania
MMIII

Library of Congress Cataloging-in-Publication Data

Plank, Robert.
George Orwell's guide through Hell : a psychological study of 1984 / by Robert Plank ; edited by Robert Reginald. — Rev. ed.
p. cm. — (The Milford series. Popular writers of today, ISSN 0163-2469 ; v. 41)
Includes bibliographical references and index.
ISBN 0-89370-313-3 (cloth). — ISBN 0-89370-413-X (pbk.)
1. Orwell, George, 1903-1950. Nineteen eighty-four. 2. Orwell, George, 1903-1950—Knowledge—Psychology. 3. Psychology in literature. I. Reginald, Robert. II. Title. III. Series.
PR6029.R8N655 1994 94-30950
823'.912—dc20 CIP

REVISED EDITION

CONTENTS

DEDICATION

Dr. Robert Plank
(1907-1983)

This book is dedicated to all of Robert Plank's friends who helped him during difficult times of serious illness and made it possible for him to finish this book. Their encouragement gave him the strength to persevere in a task which at times seemed almost insurmountable. Special thanks go to Dr. Franz Rottensteiner, who arranged for German publication, to my brother, Leopold Spire, who translated the manuscript into German, to Dr. John A. McKinnon, who helped with final proofreading, and to Robert Reginald, who edited the book. Robert Plank had the satisfaction of knowing that he had completed his most cherished work.

—Emma K. Plank

A GEORGE ORWELL CHRONOLOGY

1903 Eric Arthur Blair born June 25 at Motihari, Bengal, India, son of Richard Walmesley Blair and Ida Mabel Limouzin.

1904 Returns to England with his mother.

1917 Attends Eton (through 1921).

1922 Joins the Imperial Indian Police, and is posted to Burma.

1927 Resigns his commission while on leave to Europe.

1928 Goes to Paris (Spring) to write.

1929 Returns to England (December).

1933 *Down and Out in Paris and London* is published under the name "George Orwell," one of a half-dozen possible pseudonyms proposed by Blair to his publisher.

1934 *Burmese Days* is published. Blair works in a London bookshop, Booklovers' Corner (until 1935), where he meets many well-known literary figures.

1935 *A Clergyman's Daughter* is published.

1936 Blair marries Eileen Maud O'Shaughnessy (June 9); the marriage is childless. *Keep the Aspidistra Flying* is published. The author goes to Spain (Dec. 26), where he joins the Republican side in the Spanish Civil War.

1937 *The Road to Wigan Pier* is published. Blair returns to England (June).

1938 *Homage to Catalonia* is published.

1939 Richard Blair, Orwell's father, dies (June 28). *Coming Up for Air* is published.

1940 *Inside the Whale and Other Essays* is published. Orwell joins the Home Guard (June 12) as a Sergeant.

1941 The author attempts to join the British Army, but is rejected for reasons of health. He then accepts position as a BBC radio broadcaster for the government (through 1943). *The Lion and the Unicorn* is published.

1943 Ida Blair, the author's mother, dies (March 19). The author makes first notes for *Last Man in Europe*, later to become the novel, *Nineteen Eighty-Four*. He is named Literary Editor of the *London Tribune* (Nov.).

1944 Adopts a boy (June), whom he names Richard Horatio Blair.

1945 Eileen Blair dies during a routine operation (Mar. 29). *Animal Farm* is published, and becomes Orwell's first success.

1946 *Critical Essays* is published.

1947 The author retires to Barnhill on the island of Jura to work on *Nineteen Eighty-Four* (Spring), and finishes a first draft. Later in the year he is hospitalized for seven months (beginning on Dec. 25) for tuberculosis. *The English People* is published.

1948 Finishes final draft of *Nineteen Eighty-Four* (Nov.).

1949 *Nineteen Eighty-Four* is published to much acclaim, and shows evidence of becoming a continuing bestseller. Orwell marries Sonia Brownell on Oct. 13, but his health continues to decline.

1950 Orwell dies on Jan. 21 in Switzerland of tuberculosis; his body is returned to England for burial. *Shooting an Elephant and Other Essays* is published.

1953 *England, Your England and Other Essays* is published.

1955 The first film version of *1984* is released; Sonia Orwell later withdraws it permanently from the market.

1961 *Collected Essays* is published.

1968 *Collected Essays, Journalism, and Letters* is published.

1984 The second film version of *1984* is released to general acclaim.

INTRODUCTION

A book that has a future date in its title is like a time bomb. One day, the date that has always been hidden safely away in the future will move to the present—or to the past. And when that happens, there is an explosion—though in this case only a harmless explosion—of more books and articles that have come down on the original work like so much confetti.

This is absolutely as it ought to be. It is useful every once in a number of years to review a book, to check how it has stood the ravages of time, to see whether the ground on which it was built has shifted. Quite arbitrary dates such as the hundredth anniversary of the author's birth or the fiftieth of his death serve this same purpose. It is actually much sounder to use a date that is built into the book, such as a future date in the title (*1984* and not many others). It does not particularly detract from the value of this organic connection that the future date may have been chosen a bit casually; it is probable that Orwell hit on the ominous year by no deeper thought process than by transposing the last two digits of the year of the book's composition—from '48 into '84. As we shall see, his reach was not quite far enough. If from the thirty-six years of the interval one deducts even a minimum for the succession of wars and revolutions that culminated in the victory of Ingsoc, one is left at best with thirty years to have the brains of the people emptied and filled with new content. Even God allotted forty years for such a task.

This speedup has had certain consequences: the radical change in individuals and in their general culture as postulated by Orwell is less plausible, and some of the features of actual London in 1948 (shortages, neglected houses, occasional buzz bombs) stick to *1984* like fragments of an eggshell to the just-hatched chicken. Anthony Burgess has pounced on these chinks and made them into his own novel, *1985*, which is partly a takeoff on Orwell's *1984*: a satire on a satire.

1984 was an alternative title. Orwell's first choice was *The Last Man in Europe*[1]. I think we can be glad that with the advice and consent of his publisher he opted for the other alternative. The title *The Last Man in Europe* would have wrenched the proportion between interest in the system and interest in a victim (even if the one stands for all victims) out of equilibrium—and why "in Europe?" If it is meaningful for Winston Smith to be the last man, he must surely be the last man anywhere. One can see, though, why Orwell might have liked the title he finally rejected:

every author will want the protagonist of his story to have some distinction, even such a macabre one as being the last man, and even if only in Europe.

There is already a large secondary literature on Orwell. The standard bibliography was published in 1977. Meyers, its compiler, had to exclude a number of titles to keep the total under five hundred. Most of these, of course, are articles in journals, some are dissertations, relatively few are books. Of course, the number has grown considerably since 1977 in all these categories, and undoubtedly will continue to do so. To the mind of an inveterate admirer of Orwell (which I profess to be), the total still seems rather small for a novel that by its combination of literary merit and unique historical role deserves to be counted as one of the major books of the twentieth century.

Conscience requires, on the other hand, that one asks oneself, before inflicting yet another book about Orwell on the public: is such a book of value? I have examined the question with as much objectivity as I can muster. My answer is "yes." To justify myself, I have to state what this book shall be and what it does not intend to be. It cannot, alas, offer new information on Orwell. Highly desirable though this would be, it is probably not possible for anybody. All that has not yet been presented in the writings about Orwell is probably irretrievably lost.

This book does not intend, either, to offer interpretive criticism of Orwell's novel. It has been rightly pointed out that of all modern writers, Orwell should be the one who needs such help least. The clarity of his thought and expression means, quite simply, that one doesn't need a critic to understand Orwell.

I shall define in Chapter I what this book intends to do. Here I want to add some information that the reader should have before continuing to read this book.

Where I quote or refer to a passage of *1984*, I document it simply by putting the page number in parentheses in the text. All other references are documented by the usual notes. In referring to any source more than once, I give the full title the first time and an easily understandable abbreviation later on. In the few instances where I quote in a foreign language, I add an English translation; unless marked otherwise, these translations are mine.

Though paperback editions of *1984* are available, I have used the first American edition (New York: Harcourt, Brace and Company, Inc., 1949), a hardcover book, because this is the one most likely found in libraries. I have disregarded Orwell's expressed wish that the title of his novel be given in words (*Nineteen Eighty-Four*). I hope that his spirit will forgive me, since I quote the title so often. In referring to his papers I have used the four-volume set of *Collected Essays, Journalism and Letters of George Orwell* (*CEJL*), regardless of where the paper was originally published or in which other collection it may also be found. There are not many papers by Orwell of any significance that are not reprinted in *CEJL*, and the paperback edition of that excellent collection is still sold at a price that makes one believe that there was such a thing as the good old days.

There is, buried in the middle of *1984*, a book within the book, *The Theory and Practice of Oligarchical Collectivism*, the book that O'Brien has given Winston with the claim that Emmanuel Goldstein was its author. Later, in the torture scene, O'Brien informs Winston that the book had actually been written by several people, including himself, in the service of the Inner Party. I propose to refer to this book as "Pseudo-Goldstein."

As this is a specialized study of one work, rather than a general study of its author, there would be no need to give biographical information on Orwell. To avoid misunderstanding, though, I want to note that "George Orwell" was the penname of Eric Arthur Blair. It may also be helpful to mention that he was born in 1903 and died in January, 1950, and that *1984* was published in the summer of 1949.

Some readers will perhaps rightly feel that I owe them a programmatic statement as to what type of psychology I intend to use. If pressed for an answer, I would not proclaim any preference, but would truthfully say that I really have very little choice. The type of psychology I use is not my decision, but depends on what the various types offer. The psychology of literature deals, obviously, with products of the human mind. Branches of psychology which deal only with overt behavior cannot contribute much to its study. It does not offer much opportunity either for experimental or statistical treatment. All of this nudges me in the direction of depth psychology, but I am not aiming at proclaiming a preference for any school of psychology over another: of all of Orwell's hatreds, the one I sympathize with most enthusiastically is that of "all the smelly little orthodoxies that are now contending for our souls."[2]

Faced with the dilemma of seeming to be a male chauvinist or resorting to leathery phrases like "his/her," I shall accept the odium of appearance and shall refer to human beings by such words as "he" and "his" where gender does not matter. I think this usage (sometimes referred to as "letting the male gender embrace the female") is the least unsatisfactory solution until language develops a better way.

Now to more important matters.

This book is not written for experts, but there is one expertise that I would expect every reader to have acquired: to have read *1984*. As to other works by Orwell, I would hope that this book will stimulate reading them, but this is not a prerequisite here. To have read *1984* is needed for reading this book with understanding. Those who have read it some time ago and don't remember details should reread it before going on with this book. This is not as big a demand as it may at first glance appear. *1984* is really rather compact. It does not take much time or effort to read it even with the thorough attention it ought to be given. It may, however, take a certain emotional toil. I used to advise my students not to read *1984* in the evening unless they wanted a sleepless night. I need not have worried—they all slept well.

I finally decided it was a matter not of generations but of experience. The impact of *1984* is stronger when the reader can imagine himself living under the rule of Ingsoc. And that is easier when the reader has himself had actual experience with totalitarianism, even though none quite as vicious as Orwell's yet exists. Americans generally do not have such experiences. I personally lived in Austria, a man of the so-called Jewish race and a political opponent at that, for some three months under Nazi domination.

There are people—we might call them wise fools or foolish sages—who think that for every question of how a person should act, a fixed answer can be given once and for all. The real sages leave room for individual sensibility, for spontaneity, for acting according to the infinite variety of circumstances.

Transposing the problem from the realm of personal conduct to that of the social organization means in literary terms moving from utopias, presentations of "ideal commonwealths" where everything is regulated and all is sweetness and light, to dystopias, which state how a human society should not be run. This seeming preference for the negative has a venerable tradition, going back as far as the Ten Commandments, of which two read "thou shalt," while eight have the form "thou shalt not."[3]

Much may be said in praise of *1984*. It has been called a great book, a profound book, a wise book, an important book. Few will call it an entertaining book. I do not promise that my critique will bring any information or insight of tangible value, but hope that there are still enough people who in the tradition of George Orwell "feel strongly about prose style, love the surface of the earth, and take pleasure in solid objects and scraps of useless information."[4]

—Robert Plank

I.

PREPARING TO DESCEND INTO HELL

1.

1984, while on one level a novel of the destruction of a man, is on another level a statement of political convictions, a warning against a danger that the writer believed threatened mankind at its very heart. Like Dante centuries earlier, he guides us through hell, but the inferno he shows us is a man-made one, the product of human vices and follies.

Among the questions reasonably to be raised about that descent into hell are two weighty ones:

A. Why did Orwell choose just this type of hell; in other words, why did he think this danger to mankind the one that most needed guarding against?

B. Does he give a fair description of hell, or does he, due to some "hangup" of his own, describe hell as more infernal than it need be?

The purpose of this book is to contribute psychological observations which may help answer question B. Question A. can be more easily answered right here.

Totalitarianism is not now generally perceived as one of the great dangers we face. We frown at it as a pestilential state of affairs prevalent somewhere far away, in countries that are relatively small and not terribly important. While our government supports some of those regimes, we feel little responsibility for them. We do not think of them as threats to us. There are, of course, two very large totalitarian regimes, of which one is more or less our friend, the other our enemy. It sometimes seems as though our government has had eyes and ears and money for nothing but that enmity. The comparison of our relationship to the two makes clear that the fact of their being totalitarian does not really matter very much as such.

It is quite different with the danger of nuclear war. This, we know, may come at any moment. How shall we account for Orwell's apparent lack of concern for a nuclear holocaust? In fact he was concerned, but he could hardly be expected to make one novel shoulder the entire burden of the evils besetting mankind. He had written about the atomic bomb in magazine articles as early as August, 1945. He wrote about it again in October, 1945, and also later.[1] He incorporated in *1984* his prediction that the major powers would eventually arrive at a tacit understanding to keep the threat of atomic war alive, but to avoid war itself as too dangerous for their own survival. This state of affairs is not too different from the one we actually have. Furthermore, the situation in the late Forties and the way it was perceived then was quite different from what it has now become. The atomic raids on Hiroshima and Nagasaki were clearly of a more sinister quality than any that had gone before, but still it was possible to point out that earlier attacks had unleashed firestorms (in Dresden, and in Tokyo) that had killed almost as many people and in almost as many gruesome ways. With the two Japanese cities that fell victim to the first and so far only atomic attacks eliminated, the world seemed to continue on its wobbly course as before. It was equally possible to believe that there would be no more atomic wars, or that at the least mankind would somehow muddle through as it had done so often before. The confrontation between the fans and skeptics of technology meant a dispute between those who proudly hailed the new invention, and those who wanted to be sure that it would only be used for peaceful purposes. By now, of course, many of these supporters have come around to the position of the earlier skeptics. The "wisdom" of the governments of the U.S. and the Soviet Union during the same period increased the likelihood of atomic war, and made certain that if it came, it would be immensely more destructive. The danger of nuclear war dwarfed all other threats to mankind with an intensity that Orwell could not foresee, simply because nobody in his day could. It recent years, the collapse of the Soviet Union has somewhat abated that threat, although the continuing existence of thousands of nuclear devices still poses a long-term threat, unless they can systematically be eliminated.

2.

Similar considerations apply to ecology. Orwell was not blind to dangers posed by the degradation of the environment. In fact, the last of his four "realistic" novels that precedes *1984*[2] is on one level a novel of a man's fight both for and against his childhood memories. But just as the nuclear *djinn* had not revealed themselves in their true monstrosity in Orwell's day, so too had the destroyers of the ecology not yet shown what they could do. The protagonist of *Coming Up for Air* had as a boy watched the large and placid old fish swimming in a pond which was later converted into a dump. Orwell was among the first to see the ominous signs now evident to any participant of modern civilization. But it is hard to imagine how anybody in that day could have envisaged the full potential of environmental disaster. Now, thanks to the successful cooperation of business and government, we are faced with the possibility that the whole surface of the earth, which Orwell loved so, will eventually be converted into a chessboard of dumps, dead forests, and dried-up prairies, with a few smokestacks still belching black clouds against a leaden sky for the winds to disperse, and from which will be squeezed an occasional raindrop laden with enough sulfuric acid to make sure that life cannot get a new hold.

Lamentations of this sort often appear elitist and frivolous, and never more so than at a time when some improvement in pollution control is a side effect of the collapse of our basic industries. At this writing nobody can say whether there will ever be a recovery from that breakdown, or whether the cycle of recession and inflation is in truth but a manifestation of an ongoing change in the world economy, in some sense a reversal of the industrial revolution and its continuing conversion into an information revolution.[3]

Here again, Orwell did not foresee such a radical change from an industrial to a post-industrial society, any more than his contemporaries did. However, this development fits remarkably well with the general tenor of his predictions, at least to the extent that we can take Pseudo-Goldstein as expressing his own views. The present economic revolution appears to be heading toward that land of Cockaigne (of long-established folk imagination) where economic activity consists exclusively of consumption, while production just seems to happen without observable work. This is one of those gifts from the fairies who lead men astray: the expected blessing will actually become a curse. We perceive it now as a permanent loss of jobs, particularly in the blue-collar sector. Within the world of Orwell's ideas it has an even more sinister meaning. Pseudo-Goldstein maintains that one powerful force driving mankind into the trap of totalitarianism will be the political solution of the problem of overproduction.[4] The present economic development, if it should turn out to be as radical as it increasingly appears, would play into the hands of these pernicious forces. This would make *1984* even more topical.

Far be it from me, however, to support Orwell's opinions just because he stated them. While I believe that he was justified in relegating the dangers of nuclear war and of ecological disaster to second and third places behind the danger of totalitarianism, I cannot say the same for his attitude toward the population explosion.

He either did not see the problem or made light of it, praising philoprogenitivity and blaming people for slackness in this field. Modern opinion tends in the opposite direction. The discrepancy is partly explained by the fact that the population explosion was not as urgent a problem then as now, just as the fight against nuclear war and ecological collapse did not then require the high priorities they must have now. It is also true that more children must have seemed a reasonable counterbalance in Great Britain to the bloodletting of World War II. Still, these explanations may not totally suffice. It would seem quite probable that Orwell was motivated or mismotivated by his gnawing feeling that he was sterile. He firmly believed it, and we must assume that it was probably true. He and his wife adopted a child, and on this boy he lavished all the love he was capable of. His relation to his adopted son, Richard, was evidently the warmest of all the relationships in his life.

3.

So he had done his part personally. He could devote himself to a book on that special hell he considered the most threatening. There was no technical difficulty: *1984* is a specimen of a genre that has existed for centuries—utopias. It was only relatively recently that dysto-pias (*i.e.*, cautionary tales presenting undesirable imaginary societies) gained ascendency over *eu*topias (traditional "ideal commonwealths"). The problems of literary technique were essentially the same. Orwell found the type ready-made. *1984* is merely more grimly dystopian than any previous dystopia. We can then formulate the thrust of this study.

Any but the most insensitive reader of *1984* will put the book down with a sense of despair. Orwell describes a regime that is truly intolerable, so we tend to think that it should also be improbable; but he argues that, on the contrary, it will be inevitable. And his argument sounds cogent. As long as we are under the spell of the book, we are compelled to believe that this is our future. We naturally resist the idea. The world that Orwell depicts is so horrible, so abhorrent, that we feel it cannot, must not be true. We ask: is there any reason to think, to hope, to believe that somewhere, somehow Orwell was mistaken? Did he see things blacker than the facts warranted? Any source of such error would have to be in his mind, so we apply the psychology of literature to the work, even though its findings are generally more suggestive than conclusive. We hope to find some "hang-up" in Orwell which might reassure us that he did indeed distort his observations. This could be convincing if it can be explained why he did so.

Although this sounds like a thoroughly unscientific approach, the truth is, however, that every scientist, scholar, or explorer starts his quest with a preconceived idea of what he hopes to find. The difference between the proper and the improper researcher is not that the former has no such idea, but that the proper researcher accepts the results of his work even if they dash his hopes, while the improper one tries to bend them to his wishes. So we shall pursue the search for emotional factors in Orwell's make-up until we can be reasonably sure how they may have influenced his outlook. We can then say, with Dante, in concluding our voyage through hell, "*E quindi uscimmo a riveder le stelle*" ("Thence we emerged to see again the stars").

II.

WHO IS WINSTON SMITH?

It was clear to Orwell from the days of his early adolescence that he would become a writer. By that he meant, in the early days, that he would write bulky "realistic" novels, works that aim at giving a fictional but truthful picture of people as they are mirrored in their society. They would bring him fame.

He did write four such novels, but they did not bring him fame or money, and, in fact, scarcely anybody would be interested in them today except for the fact that we can see in them some of the ideas and images which he was later to develop into the quite different works in which his fame is grounded.

These four novels are very different in plot and mood than the later books, but similar in certain basic features. Each has one protagonist whose external adventures and (above all) whose inner processes are described with loving penetration. Each has a fairly large number of other characters, as such novels must, but it is clear that none of them is of real interest to the author in or for himself or herself; they were invented only to provide the indispensable environment for the protagonist. This already makes clear to the reader, and presumably to Orwell himself, that he was writing the novel for the sake of that central figure; there always was a special relationship between the novelist and the principal character created by him, though we do not as yet know the nature of that special relationship. It is, in any case, not the relationship so frequently found in popular novels, where the hero is often nothing but a flattering self-portrait of the author. None of the four protagonists is of such a nature that we could possibly call him the novel's hero. Their personalities are hardly even strong enough to be referred to as anti-heroes.

John Flory of *Burmese Days*, the earliest of the four novels, becomes enmeshed in intrigues that he innocently begins with the noblest of intentions, is then deprived of the chance to marry the only available girl, and ends up shooting himself. Dorothy Hare, *The Clergyman's Daughter* of the book of that title, has no way of escaping from servitude to her father but amnesia. She finally recovers her identity with all of its burdens, and then resumes the way of life that drove her out of her mind in the first place. The only real difference is that she loses her faith in the process, so that everything becomes even more intolerable than before. The central character of *Keep the Aspidistra Flying* tries to break out of his routine existence, but proves incapable of either fighting or ignoring the "money god," and finally accepts the solution of marriage, fatherhood, and the job that he had so insistently tried to avoid.

These three protagonists have several features in common: they are decent persons, of good but weak will, ineffectual, unhappy, unlucky, and natural losers and victims. George Bowling in *Coming Up for Air* has these same features, but his outstanding characteristic is a different one, fitting the different action of this fourth and last of Orwell's "realistic" novels. Here the action befits the character, since it develops out of it. It can be said of the three previous novels that they had centered on the tension between the individual (the protagonist) and society; the individual did not change much in the process, and society not at all. This, of course, was to become the basic matrix of *1984*. In *Coming up for Air*, however, society has changed very much, though the alteration has occurred prior to the start of the novel. No change occurs during the short time represented by the novel itself. The main thrust of the work is to contrast the society of the protagonist's adulthood to the society of his childhood, much to the latter's advantage. So a new motif is added to Orwell's repertoire as a novelist, the protagonist's search for his lost childhood. Like most enterprises that Orwell's characters embark on, it is a failure.

Orwell could have moved in various directions from here. In fact he chose to give up the "realistic" novel, but kept the cluster of characteristics of the protagonists he had developed, and used them to form his last and most important protagonist, Winston Smith. Smith is the most miserable and long-suffering of all of Orwell's central figures, the one we identify as the fundamental prototype of the Orwellian protagonist, distilled in such purity that it is not as difficult to understand him as it is to feel true sympathy for him, to say nothing of empathy.

When Orwell published his four "realistic" novels, he could see—and the more he wrote the more clearly he saw—that these books wouldn't in themselves bring him either fame or a living wage. To counter this, and to provide himself with extra income, Orwell consciously developed his non-fiction writing, producing an increasing number of book reviews, other journalistic works, essays, and three original books. These provided him with a forum for his observations and views on the important events and features of his time. They were not, however, strictly objective reports: each contained a considerable element of autobiography. *Down and Out in Paris and London* was not a sociological survey of the life of the underclass of those two great cities in the tradition of Mayhew and the Webbs, but a personal description of that life as Orwell himself had lived it. *The Road to Wigan Pier* was written to fulfill a commission to travel to the North of England and to study the life of the unemployed there. The manuscript that he delivered to his publisher consisted of two parts: one, his observations, for which he had been hired, so to speak, and which pleased the publisher; and two, a long autobiographical report on how he had come to hold the opinions that informed the first part, and what had convinced him that certain other people who had arrived at the same opinions much earlier were undesirable. This part, unsurprisingly, did not please his publisher. Rather magnanimously, the publishing house finally brought out the book as Orwell had submitted it, though with a preface by its president that was in essence a disclaimer of its second part. *Homage to Catalonia*, the third of these nonfiction works, was a book of passion in both senses of the word: it was written by a man who had suffered through the events recounted in it. Orwell had fought on the side of the Spanish Republic, was shot through the neck, was persecuted by the faction on his side of the war that predominated, and then barely escaped back to England.

The impressions that the reader of any or all of these works will form of Orwell's personality, talent, and character may vary widely. The impression of himself that Orwell transmits through the autobiographical parts of the writings mentioned above, and even more frankly in his autobiographical writings, notably the essay "Such, Such Were the Joys," have much more inner consistency, but are also overwhelmingly unfavorable, at least as far as his abilities are concerned (he blames himself much less explicitly for moral shortcomings). He views himself as strikingly similar to the composite character of the protagonists of his novels, and these, as we have seen, are the only characters about whom he really wrote.

Naturally, there is a difference between the character of an actual living person and the personality of a literary character. What may be self-perceived or outwardly expressed in the living person becomes in the literary character achieved fact. The living person may—as Orwell certainly did—have a tendency to humiliate or debase himself, while the literary character is merely humiliated. Orwell professed a desire to disappear in the womb of the earth, to "go down, down," while the literary character may evince the effects of following that urge.

Both the living and the literary character may be driven by a strong, overriding feeling—in our area of interest, a feeling of guilt. And the origins of that feeling may or may not be clear. Attempts may or may not be made to explain it, and they may or may not be successful.

If Orwell had purposely arranged things to make them as difficult for himself as possible, it is doubtful whether his life would have been much different from what it was. He seemed to have an uncanny talent for standing at a crossroads and choosing the less favorable turn. Though he was presumably often unaware of this tendency, it sometimes became so obvious that even he felt the need to explain it, and then he always expressed feelings of guilt. But guilt for what? For having allowed himself to be a tool of "dirty imperialism" in his five years as a police officer in Burma? But why had he taken that job initially? Presumably He was trying to expiate some guilt incurred much earlier, long before a time when conscious memory could point an accusing finger at the fact. Alas, just at this point where the matter promises to become interesting, we must let go of it, since we can not do it justice without reviewing the story of the younger sister and the robbed chocolate, which we will leave for later.

There are several narrative methods from which an author can choose if he faces the problem of what form to give to the contents of his planned novel. He is actually more likely not to construct his work so coolly, but to decide on content and form in one and the same creative act. For the purpose of analysis, however, it is convenient to look at form and content separately. The classical novels of the nineteenth century aimed at giving a picture of a whole society, and also increasingly tended to provide penetrating insights into the inner processes of its characters. Their method employed the omniscient narrator, who would present the shifting scenes, understand everything that went on in the minds of the characters, and tell the reader as much of it as he chose. This was the technique that Orwell employed in his first novel, *Burmese Days*. He did not return to it in his "realistic" novels, though he used it, and with excellent effect, in *Animal Farm*. The opposite of this form is the first person narrator, who relates only what he has personally witnessed—*i.e.*, perceived, thought, felt—leaving us the problem of figuring out from the clues he provides what is going on in the minds of the other persons in the story.

In most of his narrative fiction, and especially in *1984*, Orwell used an intermediate method: the author-narrator; but although the narrator is outside the action himself and could in principle report the actions of all the characters from the outside, with or without also revealing their inside processes, he actually presents one character, the protagonist, as though he were inside him. He tells his readers about this one character's thinking and feelings with no less intimacy than if he were writing a first-person narrative, while presenting all the other characters merely from the outside. The method reaches its purest form in *1984*. There is no scene, however short, in which Winston Smith is not present. We learn about his thoughts and feelings directly; we do not have to find out what they are from what he says or how he acts. With all the other actors the opposite is true: there are wide stretches of the novel where they are not present; we are never told directly what they think and feel; we have to form our opinions from what they say or how they act or what Winston says about them. They are like trees that form a background to a portrait of Winston—silent, perhaps meaningful, ornaments.

One result is that we are never in doubt about what goes on in Winston's mind except to the extent that he might want to mislead us, or that he might not be aware of what really goes on within him; we can, on the other hand, never be quite sure what goes on inside the other characters, or in some important instances, even about external events, insofar as Winston is not witness to them. On the rather crucial question of Winston's and Julia's mutual betrayal of each other, for instance, we know exactly how Winston "betrayed" Julia—we have been present, we have learned in every detail not only what he did, but also how he felt about it and judged himself; but insofar as Julia's betrayal of Winston is concerned, we merely hear what Winston says about it, and we note that Julia with a brief nod of her head admits that there was a betrayal; we do not learn what it was.

Let us now pull together what we have discovered about Orwell's central literary characters: they all show great similarities with each other; they also equally strongly resemble the picture that Orwell gives of himself, and to a large extent his actual character insofar as we can determine it from studying his life. His interest as a novelist is in every instance limited to the one central character of his novel, while the other characters exist merely as backdrops for the protagonist. The conclusion is inescapable: Winston Smith is the person that Orwell thought he would have been if he had had the unspeakable misfortune of living under a regime like that which rules Oceania in the world of *1984*.

It is but one step from here to the much more sweeping assumption that some critics have made, namely that the entire world of *1984* is nothing more than a fantasy spun for the sole purpose of providing proper backdrop for the figure of Winston Smith, who is really Orwell in disguise. In contrast to this interpretation, which seems to me baseless and unsupportable, it is more reasonable to presume that Orwell described *1984* in the way he did because the world he observed around him forcefully led him to believe that this was how our future could look—indeed, would look if we did not defend ourselves against it in time—and that he chose to present that detestable regime by showing what it would do to one man, volunteering in a sense to be the guinea pig on which it would be demonstrated.

III.

THE GHOSTLY BELLS OF LONDON

The plot of *1984* is deceptively simple. The author presents the picture of an execrable regime which by the year 1984 has overrun England and indeed the world. He does so by showing the fate of one man who is inexorably crushed by the system. It is hardly possible to doubt, from the very beginning of the action, that he must fail. There is little suspense.

If *1984* were a utopia like any other, that would be all. However, every page, every sentence reveals to us new details that form the picture of this horrendous imagined society, simultaneously reverberating with resonances from the protagonist's inner life, with echoes from his past. We may leave open for the moment the problem of the extent to which we can speak of a past that actually was, or of a past that Smith never experienced. On the level of the manifest action of the novel (it is of such monotonous simplicity that we can hardly call it a plot), every step results inexorably in the next. On the less obvious level of the novel's real emotional content, each step is vibrant with the resonances of memories and fantasies, and with the symbols and relics of a strange world dredged up from the unconscious, a world that in a sense becomes the real novel; it never fails to shine through the rigid frame of its external events, as an interpreted dream. Thus, *1984* is really two novels: the manifest one that is grist for the mills of the political apologist, and the hidden one that provides a psychological case study of its protagonist. The official Chinese interpretation of the book as nothing but a satire on Stalinism, or at most on the Cultural Revolution and perhaps the "Gang of Four," concerns the manifest novel; interpretations such as the one penned by Anthony West soon after *1984* was published, which treats the work as an exudation of the "hidden wound" which had warped Orwell's character—and with it his judgment—refer to what we have called the hidden novel. It is true in both areas that some interpretations are correct or at least reasonable, and that others are merely bizarre or even outrageously false. In my view, the Chinese interpretation makes no more sense than does West's, but it is useful to keep in mind that the Chinese version considers aspects which we need not deal with here further, while we cannot completely avoid dealing with West's critical views, since they have been quoted by many later critics.

To do so, we must find some way to gauge Orwell's emotional involvement in his novel. Our assumption or conclusion that Orwell depicted in Smith the person he thought he would have been had he actually lived in Oceania, is only a beginning, no more. Orwell's emotional involvement in the book needs to be studied further.

Orwell could not get a typist to come to his hermitage on the secluded Scottish island of Jura. He could not seem to get the point across that the trip from London took only forty-eight hours if connections were good, and that, although his house was isolated, one could quite easily walk eight miles to the nearest store or a restaurant. So he typed much of *1984* himself, most of it in bed. His letters are full of complaints about his poverty, the pernicious weather, the poor food, his bad health, and the difficulties of writing in such an environment. It is almost as if he had sought such a refuge to imbue his growing manuscript with the grimness of his surroundings, and the knowledge of his deteriorating health. One can imagine that the writer would thus press the last ounce of strength out of his fingers in a desperate race against the Grim Reaper, so as to give form to something of such overriding emotional importance to him that he would not be able to depart from this Earth in peace before he had written it. A book reviewer friend of mine recently told me that he shared the opinion of many, including C. S. Lewis,[1] that *Animal Farm* is a better book than *1984*, but added that "I still can't deny the power that *1984* has over me, a malevolent intensity few books have."[2] It may be more reasonable to assume that this power results from the wrestling with death than from a hidden wound suffered long, long before.

One thing that Winston Smith cannot complain of is a lack of problems or worries. From the moment on that April day when the clocks are striking thirteen,[3] when he embarks on his self-destructive career of "thoughtcrime," to that other afternoon when we take our leave from him in the Chestnut Tree Café, when he can no longer hope for anything but for the bullet to enter his brain,[4] he suffers. He is not always a passive sufferer: though he does nothing to resist his fate, he has a knack for bringing down disaster on his own head, which he does to perfection.

All sorts of practical difficulties beset him, from the rustiness of his razor blades to the neighbors' intolerable brats. These difficulties, attacks, and humiliations wear him down; but they would be tolerable were it not for the choking atmosphere that pervades the world of *1984*: the constant surveilance, the ever-present intimation of being swept, utterly helpless, toward some preordained destruction. Winston is a sufferer, but unlike Homer's Odysseus, the "divine sufferer" who becomes a tragic figure, Smith remains merely pitiable.

He cannot change the course of events, except to bring the final catastrophe closer. He himself knows this, though at times he deceives himself about this and many other things. There is no comfort for him in the present, no hope in the future. The only defense left to Winston is to dredge up the past and to find gratification in exploring it. It does not matter whether these chunks of his earlier life are jewels or rubbish, real or imagined. The only time he minds is when the dredge fails to bring up anything. We hear about this as early as the third page of the novel:

> He tried to squeeze out some childhood memory that should tell him whether London had always been quite like this....But it was no use, he could not remember: nothing remained of his childhood except a series of bright-lit *tableaux*, occurring against no background and mostly unintelligible.[5]

Sometimes his search is rewarded, but only with illusion:

> All the while that they were talking the half-remembered rhyme kept running through Winston's head: Oranges and lemons, say the bells of St. Clements, You owe me three farthings, say the bells of St. Martins! It was curious, but when you said it to yourself you had the illusion of actually hearing bells, the bells of a lost London that still existed somewhere or other, disguised and forgotten. From one ghostly steeple after another he seemed to hear them pealing forth. Yet so far as he could remember he had never in real life heard church bells ringing.[6]

He will not shrink from any absurdity if only he can complete his knowledge of those nursery rhymes. He is told the end:

> Here comes a candle to light you to bed,
> Here comes a chopper to chop off your head,

but he heeds no warning:

> ...there must be another line after the bells of Old Bailey. Perhaps it could be dug out of Mr. Charrington's memory, if he were suitably prompted.[7]

One of the great turning points of the novel comes when Winston and Julia visit O'Brien to join "the Brotherhood," the allegedly secret underground organization that fights the Party. Eventually we discover that the Brotherhood probably does not exist. The deceit initiating Winston and Julia into the nonexistent opposition is the deadliest part of the trap that will be sprung on them. But since the characters do not know this (neither does the reader), this does not detract from the somber solemnity of the occasion. Winston and Julia declare their willingness to do practically anything in the service of the Brotherhood: to murder, to spread venereal disease, to throw acid into the faces of children, to commit suicide—and all that without ever having seen any results of their struggle, which will at best bear fruit in a hundred years.

At the end O'Brien asks whether there is anything they want to say before they go, any message, any question? Winston ponders this, then asks:

> Did you ever happen to hear an old rhyme that begins: Oranges and lemons, say the bells of St. Clements?

It undoubtedly takes O'Brien's considerable self-control to complete the stanza "with a sort of grave courtesy," and to add nothing more critical than, "And now, I am afraid, it is time for you to go."[8]

Winston has taken a step from the sublime to the ridiculous with the bravura of an innocent child. It is virtually a *cliché* to speak of a face so ugly that only a mother could love it, and since we might think of an author as the parent of the characters he invents, we might well wonder whether Orwell could have continued to love Winston Smith (if he ever did) when he engaged in antics such as this. The poetry of the ghostly bells, though somewhat removed from reality, gives Winson a gloriole; the insistence on getting every one of these rhymes, however inappropriate to the occasion, takes it away. The question here is not whether persons who go so far to satisfy their obsession exist in reality—if they don't, the reality of *1984* could conceivably have brought them into existence, or Orwell could have erroneously imagined that it would have. This is not what could have engaged Orwell's willingness to sacrifice his last bit of strength. Its intensity also could not have come from his interest in Winston Smith. However close Winston may have come in some context to representing his author, he remains too small a man, without the spark of fire necessary to inflame anyone's—even the author's—passionate interest. That intensity could only have come from Orwell's deep feeling against the system. The hatred of the government whose operations are conducive to the development in the otherwise-not-very-interesting Winston of such folly, that dislike must have been the severe driving force that made Orwell write the way he did—that, rather than any empathy with Winston, however much he may in certain respects have been Orwell's merely somewhat distorted self-portrait. For if there is one thing we can be sure of, it is that Orwell was not in love with any portrait of himself. Thus we can dispose of West's theory of the "hidden wound."

Because Winston is the person that Orwell felt he would have been if he had had to live in his *1984*, Smith is a distorted self-portrait of himself. And because of this distortion, Orwell could not live in peace with it. He must continually improve its traits, providing more and more of a nonexistent past to give Smith a more convincing identity. So Winston is compelled to dig up anything which can serve as his past. He does not enjoy this quest, but he has to do it.

There are people, both in reality and in fiction, who live in peace with their memories; their reflections arise spontaneously, offering themselves for their owners' enjoyment. There are others who do not so much own their memories as are owned by them. They are compelled to regenerate them, but they cannot enjoy the results of their efforts, which can at best be useful to them. Some can dredge up such memories themselves, others need the help of a psychoanalyst. If their memories come up unbidden or are brought up without proper skill and peace of mind, they degenerate into the psychological equivalent of painful ulcers. So Winston keeps searching for the missing rhymes, but finding them does not relieve his tension. He is not happier when he finds the missing lines from the nursery rhyme. His search leads nowhere, but it must go on.

The reason that such an obsession is plausible in *1984* when it might not be as plausible in the real world, is that in *1984* the search for the individual past and the historic past coincide. We live in a world where the history of an individual's emotional development is often hidden from his awareness by repression, while the external events of his environment and the facts of his own existence remain accessible to his memory and can be reconstructed by him from physical records or from what he learns from others. It is the peculiarity of the regime that Orwell imagined for *1984* that the general, collective past is concealed by amnesia; its reconstruction is "thoughtcrime," the most heinous crime of Orwell's imagined world. The citizens of that regime are first prohibited, and then effectively prevented, from knowing or remembering what happened in the world during their lifetime.

The system works only too well, as Winston finds out when he tries to explore what things were like before the revolution by the seemingly simple device of asking his elders.[9] The passages recording the dismal failure of "oral history" are remarkable for two reasons: they beautifully parody such endeavors, incidentally showing, as had *Animal Farm*, what delicious humor Orwell could write when his passions did not block its flow. The beauty of the parody is much enhanced by the absence of rancor: the people parodied include himself, for he had engaged in such interviewing on his trip to the North of England some years previously, and the report of that research, combined with a second part that was autobiographical and polemical, formed his 1936 book, *The Road to Wigan Pier*.[10] Secondly, the passage establishes the connection, deep in the unconscious, between guilt and punishment. In trying to unearth the past, Winston has, by the standards of *1984*, sinned. So what happens when circumstances compel him to terminate his sinful escapade? He "hardly noticed when his feet carried him out into the street again."[11] Promptly they carry him to where his unconscious directs them: "He seemed to know the place. Of course! He was standing outside the junk shop where he had bought the diary."[12] He "had sworn never to come near the place again." It is the place where he will buy the paperweight, where he will rent the room, where he will be arrested. He has sinned and he will make sure that he is punished. It is notable, though, that the sin this time does not consist of an infraction of rules accepted by him: he has transgressed against a rule set up by the power of the state; he has defied an authority that ruled over him before he even had a chance to internalize its demands.

These laws are no less strong for that, and their violation brings a feeling of guilt that cannot be ascribed to reason. Thus, only meaningless and severely distorted fragments of the past can emerge from Winston's subconscious, like those capitalists with their top hats; and it is only natural that Winston's personal childhood memories are equally fragmented. Hence his complaint that his efforts to remember his childhood produce nothing but "a series of bright-lit tableaux, occurring against no background and mostly unintelligible."[13]

One of the more brightly-lit *tableaux* is that of the murderous fight for a piece of chocolate. He was ten or twelve at the time, his sister two or three (Orwell had a sister five years his junior). He remembers "above all, the fact that there was never enough to eat."[14] One day his father disappeared. This is evidently as usual in Oceania as it was in Argentina during the military regime, a regime with which, former President Reagan noted, we shared certain values. So her husband's disappearance does not surprise Winston's mother, but it does dispirit her. "For hours at a time she would sit almost immobile on the bed, nursing his young sister," who was ailing, "with a face made simian by thinness."[15] "It was evident even to Winston that she was waiting for something that she knew must happen,"[16] and when she took Winston into her arms and pressed him against her for a long time, which happened only "very occasionally," he knew "that this was somehow connected with the never-mentioned thing that was about to happen."[17]

It eventually did happen, under unusual circumstances. The mother's tendency to be more giving to the young sister did not extend to food. "She took it for granted that he, 'the boy,' should have the biggest portion; but however much she gave him he invariably demanded more....One day a chocolate ration was issued....Winston heard himself demanding in a loud booming voice that he should be given the whole piece."[18] After a long and of course fruitless argument, his mother made the more than Solomonic decision that he would get three quarters of the piece, the little girl one-quarter, and she herself nothing. This did not help. "Then with a sudden swift spring he had snatched the piece of chocolate out of his sister's hand and was fleeing for the door."[19] A futile exchange of words and gestures ends with the mother drawing her arms around the girl and pressing the girl's face against her breast. "Something in the gesture told him that his sister was dying."[20] When he came home a few hours later "his mother had disappeared" (so had his sister, but in the *résumé* of the events that he gives to himself and to Julia he does not mention this). At the time he remembers all this, he has no way of knowing whether they are alive or dead, but has every reason to presume the latter.

The story is brought into Winston's consciousness by a dream, but we are not told anything about the dream except that Winston woke up from it "with his eyes full of tears."[21] He tried to tell Julia, who was sleeping beside him, about it but found it too complex, especially because "a memory connected with it had swum into his mind in the few seconds after waking."[22] This, of course, is the memory of the chocolate episode. He associates with the final gesture of his mother pressing his sister to herself another gesture "made again thirty years later by the Jewish woman he had seen on the news film, trying to shelter the small boy from the bullets, before the helicopters blew them both to pieces."[23] He introduces the chocolate story to Julia with a somewhat cryptic remark: "'Do you know,' he said, 'that until this moment I believed I had murdered my mother?'"[24]

We are not told whether it was the dream or something else that disabused him, but it was in any event a change toward rationality. As he tells the story, it seems apparent that his mother would have disappeared anyway and his sister would have died anyway. But the turn toward rationality does not go deep: the guilt remains, with the result that Winston feels that the punishment which he eventually suffers is in some way deserved. This, and the fact that this fragment of Winston's memory is very "bright-lit" indeed, may well lead us to the hypothesis that we are here dealing with one of Orwell's own memories. It seems likely that he is recalling something he did as a child to his mother and his younger sister which lent itself to imaginative reworking into a memory of Winston. We do not know enough of Orwell's childhood to verify or refute our hunch or to specify what that event may have been. If it was anything similar to the chocolate episode, the similarity certainly must have been limited. Orwell's mother did not disappear— whatever happened in Orwell's childhood happened in England in the early part of the century, not in Argentina in its later part—and his younger sister survived him.

If there is a genuine memory of Orwell's behind the memory of Winston, it is a screen memory, a memory of something which happened but was not in itself of emotional importance, and which derived its apparent emotional significance from some even earlier event so laden with emotion that it had to be repressed. Working his own screen memory into Winston Smith's significant memory, Orwell the author not only changed the facts in a way that we can no longer trace them, but endowed them, along with similar events, with the power of setting the future apart from the past. Orwell heard the church bells—for Winston they are the ghostly bells of a vanished London.

When Winston and Julia visit O'Brien to join the (fictitious) Brotherhood, wine is brought in, a drink quite familiar to O'Brien but unknown to his guests, and O'Brien opens the proceedings by toasting the equally fictitious Emmanuel Goldstein. The completion of the "initiation" is to be sealed by a second toast. O'Brien tentatively proposes several possible toasts.

"What shall it be this time?" he said, still with the same faint suggestion of irony. "To the confusion of the Thought police? To the death of Big Brother? To humanity? To the future?"

Winston does not hesitate: "To the past," said Winston.[25] This is in character for Winston, but in a sense also for Orwell.

As Winston and Julia leave, O'Brien gives them small whitish pills to counteract the aroma of the wine, so no one will be able to smell it and draw dangerous conclusions. This is rational enough under the circumstances, but critics have also noted, probably correctly, that the solemn consumption of red wine and a white tablet mimics the transubstantiation, the crucial event of the Mass. It would be altogether erroneous to think of this as a parody. Orwell's attitude toward religion and specifically toward Christianity was complex and ambivalent, but by no means truly negative. He had seen in Spain a powerful church throwing its support squarely to the side of Fascism. In some of his essays, and indeed in those into which he put most of his intimate thinking, he had contrasted the attitude of saints who stress the future life and thus devalue earthly life with the "humanist" attitude that was his own, and which he found best embodied in Shakespeare. Yet he believed that the lowering of morality and standards which he thought characteristic of his age, as so many people find it characterizes ours, was due to the gradual loss of the belief in individual immortality among growing numbers of people. This was a typical middle-class complaint in the early part of the century. The usual middle-class and upper-class answer was that the mass of people (the lower classes) must be kept enthralled by religious principles (the "educated," naturally, did not need religion). Orwell does not seem ever to have considered such a solution.

He wrote about the problem explicitly in two articles, both included in Volume 3 of *The Collected Essays, Journalism and Letters of George Orwell*, from his regular column "As I Please" in the British journal *Tribune*, of March 3 and April 14, 1944 (#s 24 and 31 in the *Collection*). The latter article contains a reply to a Catholic writer who had maintained that a public opinion poll would show an overwhelming majority of Englishmen still believing in personal immortality. Orwell points out that while people indeed might tell an interviewer that they believed in life after death, the quality of that belief wasn't what it had been for our forefathers:

> Never, literally never in recent years, have I met anyone who gave me the impression of believing in the

> next world as firmly as he believed in the existence of, for instance, Australia...have you ever met a Christian who seemed as afraid of Hell as he was of cancer?[26]

So, what was to be done about it?

> I do not want the belief in life after death to return, and in any case it is not likely to return. What I do point out is that its disappearance has left a big hole, and that we ought to take notice of that fact.... [Man] is not likely to salvage civilization unless he can evolve a system of good and evil which is independent of heaven and hell.[27]

> There is little doubt that the modern cult of power worship is bound up with the modern man's feeling that life here and now is the only life there is.[28]

We either get the new ethics that takes this into account, or we get *1984*. Having written the novel which did all it could to prevent the horrendous alternative, Orwell was able to think of his soul. On his deathbed he requested that he be buried in a churchyard according to the rites of the Church of England. And so it was done.

IV.

THE CHESTNUT TREE CAFÉ

1.

The Chestnut Tree Café is the rather odd establishment where the ghostly survivors gather who have irrevocably become victims of the regime. "Corpses waiting to be sent back to the grave,"[1] they wait for the bullets that will hit their necks from behind. They do little but drink their horrid gin, listen to the radio, take a quite illusory interest in chess problems.

It is one of the few specific locations within London that are mentioned in *1984*. It may be a relic from pre-revolutionary times, but it may also be true that, with the exception of the giant white pyramids of the four departments of government which bestride the landscape like arrogant conquerors, it could be the only new building. All the other London buildings of which we hear, from the crumbling housing projects to the phony national monuments, are old edifices that have been allowed to decay and that in some cases, like the specifically named churches, have been perverted.

The Chestnut Tree Café is at the same time one of the few locations where specific, even crucial elements of the novel's action take place. It should be well worthwhile to inquire what it is, why it is named as it is, what it represents.

Two roots are easily laid bare once we decide where to look, namely at the most eminent among the Café's guests, since his patronage gave the Café its reputation, and at the music occasionally played there, which in turn explains its name and establishes its narrative function.

Jones, Aaronson, and Rutherford, whose patronage of the Chestnut Tree so impresses Winston, are big fish in comparison to him but minnows compared to the really big fish. It is said that "years and decades ago" Emmanuel Goldstein himself had been seen among the guests.[2] Goldstein is, of course, the scapegoat character in *1984*—as Snowball was in *Animal Farm*. He represents the man who in real life had been the Russian Bolshevik leader whose original name was similar to Goldstein but who is known to history under his *nom de guerre*, Leon Trotsky. It was known that while waiting for the cue that would propel him onto the him onto the stage of history, he was a steady guest of the Café Central in Vienna. The anecdote has it that Count Czernin, the Foreign Minister of the Hapsburg Monarchy, wanting to express his skepticism about the chances of revolution in Russia, said: "Oh, yeah? And who will command their armies? Herr Bronstein from the Café Central?" And that was of course exactly what happened.

The guests of the Café in Orwell's novel naturally have no such glory to look forward to. They have played their roles and lost their games. That is the difference between *1984*, the arbitrarily chosen date of the ignominous end of the revolution, and the real date, 1917, when the trumpets of history proclaimed its beginning.

But why the "Chestnut Tree"? We surely are not to imagine that such a tree would grow there, let alone "spread." The Café Central was located in the most densely built-up central part of Vienna, wall against wall, with not a tree in sight. The Café in Orwell's novel sounds more like the sort of place at which it is proverbially said that not a blade of grass will ever grow. But when the music that issues from the loudspeaker in the Chestnut Tree Café switches to its special "braying," "yellow" tone, when it becomes obviously a special message for Winston Smith, the message is:

> Under the spreading chestnut tree
> I sold you and you sold me.

Long before the sale is consummated, Winston knows what sale is meant.

In 1936, as a young man from Vienna who had never been beyond the confines of Central Europe, I made my first visit to London. Vienna had long since lost its position as one of the world's powerful cities; London's similar fate was still hidden in the womb of time. London could still consider itself, and we would still consider it, the center of the world. And the wonders that I saw there!: in the heights above the buzzing streets, in depths much deeper than provincial imagination thought, one could transact such mundane business as buying tickets and boarding trains. Leading to that astonishing underworld were the first escalators I ever saw. And at the bottom of the last escalator there was, unashamed in the crudity of its poster colors, the spreading chestnut tree. And:

> Under the spreading chestnut tree
> A glass of Guinness stood.
> The smith, a mighty man was he,
> His Guinness did him good.
> And would it do the same for me?
> My Guinness, yes, it would.

I had never heard of the *Guinness Book of World Records* (which, in any case, was not published until the 1950s). I did not know how the smith got into the act. Even though the poem burlesqued here was American rather than British, the users of the escalators evidently had learned it in school. This is what Longfellow had written:

THE VILLAGE BLACKSMITH

Under a spreading chestnut tree
The village smithy stands;
The smith, a mighty man is he,
With large and sinewy hands;
And the muscles of his brawny arms
Are strong as iron bands.

His hair is crisp, and black, and long,
His face is like the tan;
His brow is wet with honest sweat,
He earns whate'er he can,
And looks the whole world in the face,
For he owes not any man.

Week in, week out, from morn till night,
You can hear his bellows blow;
You can hear him swing his heavy sledge,
With measured beat and slow,
Like a sexton ringing the village bell,
When the evening sun is low.

And children coming home from school
Look in at the open door;
They love to see the flaming forge,
And hear the bellows roar,
And catch the burning sparks that fly
Like chaff from a threshing floor.

He goes on Sunday to the church,
And sits among his boys;
He hears the parson pray and preach.
He hears his daughter's voice,
Singing in the village choir,
And it makes his heart rejoice.

It sounds to him like her mother's voice,

Singing in Paradise!
He needs must think of her once more,
How in the grave she lies,
And with his hard, rough hand he wipes
A tear out of his eyes.

Toiling,—rejoicing,—sorrowing.
Onward through life he goes;
Each morning sees some task begin,
Each evening sees it close;
Something attempted, something done,
Has earned a night's repose.

Thanks, thanks to thee, my worthy friend.
For the lesson thou has taught!
Thus at the flaming forge of life
Our fortunes must be wrought;
Thus on its sounding anvil shaped
Each burning deed and thought!

There are certain poems that seem somehow destined to live on through parodies. The Village Smithy is one of them. The most renowned of the breweries in the British Isles apparently used it for its purpose with as little compunction as Orwell was later to use it for his.

It might be interesting to paraphrase systematically the economic and social configuration and the family structure that Longfellow offers us, but it would be unnecessary because all can be said in one sentence: the situation and way of life that Longfellow depicts for us as a model is clearly diametrically opposed to that which prevails in *1984*. And this is obviously why Orwell uses a parody of it to convey the fact that betrayal is the usual course at The Chestnut Tree.

2.

This does not, of course, necessarily mean that the picture given by Longfellow is the one Orwell would have recognized as a desirable alternative to *1984*, perhaps not even as a possible one. Pseudo-Goldstein says that it would have been impossible to return to an agricultural society.[3] That fictitious book does not necessarily reflect Orwell's own opinions, but it often does; and in this instance we can be nearly sure that it does, because there is Orwell's statement that without "a high level of mechanical development, human equality is not practically possible."[4] There are many similar passages in Orwell's essays, too numerous and diverse to be listed here, where indubitably he speaks in his own authentic voice. The world of the village smithy is a beautiful world, child of the wish more than of historical research; it would be more fittingly introduced by the fairy tale formula, "once upon a time there was," than by the scholarly formula, "research has demonstrated that in the year..." It is a world characterized by certain social and economic qualities, and also by the qualities, especially the physique, of the smith. Both fit together.

The environment, of course, is one that belongs to the past, and that even in the past was never as prevalent as nostalgia would have it: an economy of free and equal producers, nobody exploited, nobody exploiting, an unintentional grouping of small, independent enterprises embedded in a multitude of similar enterprises, quite outside the web of markets, competition, credit, and all other modern worries. Very nice, but how viable? It would perhaps produce the balm in Gilead that heals the sin-sick soul, but would it cure the ailments Orwell was concerned with? Did Orwell fail to realize how anachronistic all this was? He did not. The very heart of his grievance against the system as imagined in *1984* is the idea which he makes the starting point of the book ascribed to Goldstein: that equality and a decent life for all had been impossible as long as modern technology was not available, and that the truly unforgivable crime of the rulers of *1984* was to deny the benefits of modern technology to the people, just when they could have been widely distributed.[5] The smith in his village smithy represents a pre-industrial world still free of these modern atrocities. He is a *petit bourgeois.* It certainly seems very odd at first glance that Orwell should pick a *petit bourgeois* as a positive symbol. But we must not overlook that in the crucial initiation scene, when O'Brien proposes the toast, "To the future!," Winston replies without hesitation, "To the past!" This is not necessarily, as it might seem, an expression of a backward-looking mind. Given the fact that any change that Winston can remember as having happened in his lifetime has been to the worse, what should he favor but the past?

The smith, moreover, was a particularly ingratiating symbol of the past. Since his main business was to keep the horses shod, the smithy was central to the village in a higher degree than even the service station is now; and since the work of the smith was essentially handwork, the trade both attracted and developed "mighty" men "with broad and sinewy hands." From the middle of the eighteenth century it became increasingly clear that future wealth would be based on labor. The industrial revolution somehow did not attract art or literature very strongly: but the smith as a successor to the landowner was a more welcome motive. Longfellow was not the only artist of his day to present a smith and his smithy with sympathy overlaid with even a touch of envy and deep respect. The English nineteenth-century poet and Catholic, Gerard Manley Hopkins, wrote a poem on a blacksmith (he preferred the more archaic word "farrier") whom he called Felix Randal.[6] It is as hard to imagine the spirit of these poems surviving into the industrial era as to imagine that we will ourselves encounter a smithy like the one described by Longfellow alongside an interstate highway.

The nineteenth century was also a time when artists featured the blacksmith as a worthy subject. Goya can be taken to represent the peak of this development. Men doing a job and doing it well, the dignity of workers caught in the performance of tasks that require mastery—these were the true themes of much of Goya's best later work.[7] It was in work that Goya found the strongest intimation of the survival of man's dignity.[8] The smithy "is his only painting that is an integral whole rather than a meaningful fragment torn out of an inscrutable context."[9]

It is no coincidence that when Orwell wanted to pick a shining example of the *petit bourgeois* at his best, he did not use, say, a cobbler or a green-grocer, but foreswore originality, and repeating Longfellow's choice, picked a blacksmith. If his glorification of the *petit bourgeois* still leaves a modern reader somewhat bewildered, as we would imagine Longfellow's readers were not, the reason is perhaps that over the past century and a half the term *petit bourgeois* has assumed the character of an epithet and has almost lost the meaning it originally had, the designation of a specific social class. When Marx and Engels wrote, it seemed to them that the *bourgeois* had pretty well had its day. Developments since then have made this somewhat less certain. Orwell was not uninfluenced by the literature of his day that made less alluring the prospect of a world consisting of one employer and millions of employees of the same look. James Burnham's *The Managerial Revolution* in particular impressed him. His thoughts were nudged in the direction of considering the need to build dams against that special dirty flood.

3.

Orwell was guided in this direction by his reading, observation, and general thought, rather than by any *petit bourgeois* experiences or family tradition. His mother's father was a French colonial who grew rich as a teak merchant in Southeast Asia, and then lost money in rice speculation—not exactly the blacksmith type. Orwell's paternal ancestry included an earl. From that point down there was always a youngest son who had to be satisfied with the smallest portion from the feast; the life of the gentleman of leisure yielded over the generations to a still respectable, but hardly profitable, service to the Crown. Orwell's father was a rather low-placed and not very successful colonial employee concerned with the control of the opium trade in India and its sale to China. Great Britain had started (and naturally won) a war against that ancient empire to make certain that, however unenlightened it might remain in its internal affairs, it would certainly not try to interfere with the sacred freedom of trade. "Large and sinewy hands?" A task begun each morning, completed each evening? These were not the spiritual flowers growing on Orwell's family tree. But he might well have wished they had been. This might even be a reason why he gave the protagonist of *1984* the last name of Smith.

In any event, if he displayed anything like nostalgia for the *petit bourgeois*, it can only have been a desire to "recover" what he had never possessed, a trait rather pervasive in his character and undoubtedly indicating that he thought he would be a happier man if he had possessed it. This is perhaps the point where the miserable Winston Smith is not so far from touching the magnificent Don Quixote.

The non-existent chestnut tree for which the fateful Café is named is not the only chestnut tree in Orwell's work. George Bowling, the protagonist of *Coming Up for Air*, who in relation to Winston Smith is what the caterpillar is to the butterfly, remembers "the July nights under the chestnut tree" with his girl friend; but this may be a wistful thought of something that he wishes had happened, like the thought of the powerful men who work in the smithy; and in any case it is not important for the progression of the story in which it occurs. The Chestnut Tree Café, however, is crucial for the plot of *1984* because it is there, and because through it that Winston receives the two revelations that finally accomplish his fate: the revelation that Big Brother, the devilish divinity of *1984*, is both a jealous god and an omnipotent god, one who knows when Winston enters the Café and changes the music accordingly; and at the very end the revelation that this same god, who may have created heaven and hell but who has certainly created the very special hell which is *1984*, is also the god of universal love. His hell also was created, as Dante has put it, by "*La summa sapienza e il primo amore*" ("by highest wisdom and primordial love").

V.

THE WORLD IN THE GLOBE OF GLASS

1.

Winston Smith has an apartment in a Victory Mansion. It is sparsely furnished. He has very few personal belongings: in *1984* there is little he could have and little he could do with it. Day in, day out, he wears the prescribed blue overalls.[1] Orwell never for a moment lets us forget that in Oceania everything that a member of the Outer Party has or does is observed by the Thought Police, and that anyone who shows the slightest inclination to deviate from a very narrow path is immediately marked down for "vaporizing." Even to stroll into those parts of London where the proles live (and where a Party member in his overalls is as conspicuous as a man from Mars), to enter a store there and buy something other than, say, a razor blade, is as prudent as climbing a lightning rod during a thunderstorm.

Yet this is exactly what Winston has done, as we learn at the very beginning of the novel, when he buys a diary—that is, an empty book to use for writing a diary: a "young lady's keepsake album" as Mr. Charrington later[2] calls it, with his disarming, old-fashioned charm—plus a pen and inkpot, when he actually starts his journal.[3] This in itself is much worse than his shopping trip, and Winston knows it perfectly well.

He also makes another purchase, however, which we will now consider.

2.

Although the type of object is widely known, it does not seem to have a name. Orwell describes it thus:

> It was a heavy lump of glass, curved on one side, flat on the other, making almost a hemisphere. There was a peculiar softness, as of rainwater, in both the color and the texture of the glass. At the heart of it,

> magnified by the curved surface, there was a strange, pink, convoluted object that recalled a rose or a sea anemone...[4]

—or perhaps a piece of coral. Winston guesses that the object, presumably made more than a hundred years ago, was intended to serve as a paperweight. Without hesitation or haggling, he buys it for four dollars. The fateful diary had cost $2.50. In reading of this fairly casual purchase, we hardly get the impression that this paperweight will play a great role in Winston's life and hence in the events of the novel. And in a factual, external sense, it indeed does not. There is nothing that he will ever do with it except gaze at it, and it does nothing to him except induce reveries.

It could be said with some justification that the purchase of the paperweight is one step on Winston's self-chosen path toward perdition. But he has already initiated this with his first purchase, and he will seal his doom by renting the room above the shop where he has seen the paperweight. All this could have been done without a lump of glass. There is no narrative necessity for Orwell to introduce the object. There is even less of a need to provide Winston with it, since for him it is utterly unusable.

He has no papers to weigh down. To have any personal notes would be "crimethink." And he has no letters—there are none in *1984*:

> ...few people ever wrote letters. For the messages that it was occasionally necessary to send, there were printed postcards with long lists of phrases, and you struck out the ones that were inapplicable.[5]

One would scarcely keep enough of these to need a paperweight.

Letters today do not play the role they did before the telephone and computer E-mail were invented; as affluence spreads along with functional illiteracy, oral means of communication increasingly replace written ones. Still, it is difficult to imagine a world without letters: they have been around for such a long time. The Bible already knows of many written communications, all heavy with significance, from the letter given to Uriah to the letters of the Apostles. With the growth of civilization, mail has grown and become ever more diversified: business correspondence, Christmas cards, death notices, blackmail, love letters. But in *1984*, with so much else that makes life livable, this great invention, this inexhaustible expression of individuality, this bulwark of the private sphere, has been cut off, root and branch. Orwell's skill shows in his ability to make the readers feel overwhelmingly repelled by this aspect of a possible future society without letting them become aware of what specifically they are missing. There are no letters any more, and we have scarcely noticed.

So Winston doesn't even know about letters. He is no different in this from many millions of his contemporaries. Everyone is separated from everyone else by a gulf as unbridgeable as the gulf which separated Odysseus from Penelope. The difference is that in the world depicted by Homer, letters were not yet much used; in the world depicted by Orwell they have been abolished altogether.

Winston is not unaware of how paradoxical it is that he buys this useless object; what appeals to him about it is not so much its beauty as the air it seems to possess, of belonging to an age quite different from the present one. The soft, rain-watery glass is not like any glass that he has ever seen. The thing is doubly attractive because of its apparent uselessness, though he can guess that it must once have been intended as a paperweight.[6] To Julia's question as to what he thinks it is, he replies:

> "I don't think it's anything—I mean, I don't think it was ever put to any use. That's what I like about it. It's a little chunk of history that they've forgotten to alter. It's a message from a hundred years ago, if one knew how to read it."[7]

So he reads it his own way:

> Winston did not get up for a few minutes more. The room was darkening. He turned over toward the light and lay gazing into the glass paperweight. The inexhaustingly interesting thing was not the fragment of coral but the interior of the glass itself. There was such a depth of it, and yet it was almost as transparent as air. It was as though the surface of the glass had been the arch of the sky, enclosing a tiny world with its atmosphere complete. He had the feeling that he could get inside it, and that in fact he was inside it, along with the mahogany bed and the gateleg table and the clock and the steel engraving and the paperweight itself. The paperweight was the room he was in, and the coral was Julia's life and his own, fixed in a sort of eternity in the heart of the crystal.[8]
>
> So long as they were actually, in this room, they both felt no harm could come to them. Getting there was difficult and dangerous, but the room itself was sanctuary. It was as when Winston had gazed into the heart of the paperweight, with the feeling that it would

> be possible to get inside that glassy world, and that once inside it time could be arrested.[9]

The very dream that brings the episode of the chocolate which we discussed in Chapter III back to Winston's consciousness is softened by that magic glass:

> It was a vast, luminous dream in which his whole life seemed to stretch out before him like a landscape on a summer evening after rain. It had all occurred inside the glass paperweight, but the surface of the glass was the dome of the sky, and inside the dome everything was flooded with a clear soft light in which one could see into interminable distances.[10]

3.

It is obvious that the paperweight poses some riddles. We can try to solve them by looking for clues in comparable objects in other works of literature and art, and by considering the problems of fetishism.

Few movies had an impact so immediate and at the same time so lasting as Orson Welles's *Citizen Kane*, his thinly-disguised masterpiece film about William Randolph Hearst. To be sure, its quick fame sprang largely from the titillation we are prone to feel when a well-known and controversial person is shown without his mask, when we learn what really made him tick. Hearst was a man of burning popular interest, an almost mythical figure, who was said to have driven the United States into a war for no other purpose than to give his papers sensational scoops.

The film opens with Kane on his deathbed—not an act of kindness on the part of Welles when the real Hearst was still lustily living, but that is part of the game. Kane's last word is "Rosebud," uttered as he drops a paperweight, which shatters. A journalist looking for any tidbit of knowledge about the great man takes the word for a woman's name. Who was she? The chase for Rosebud becomes the structure of the film. Like a baying bloodhound, the reporter tries to follow her trail, thereby unrolling for us Kane's life history. But the hunt is in vain. There is no clue to what Rosebud is or was.

The more productive question would have been: *what* was Rosebud? At the end of the film, as we see Kane's many belongings being burned on a trash heap, the camera (but not the film's characters) focuses on a child's sled; as the wood flares, the flames for a moment light up the name of the manufacturer—Rosebud. Then all is destroyed, and Kane's secret with it. The ending of this film has been both criticized as pure Hollywood schmalz and much admired as symbol: this is how pomp and power will crumble, how those searching for the past must hopelessly grope, and how certain childhood experiences determine life more definitely than all those later, seemingly so much more important, events. One scholar, however, has taken the view that Rosebud itself isn't the "central symbol" of the film, but that the paperweight is.[11] One could argue forever, of course, as to which symbol is more central than the other. In any case, since Kane on his deathbed has held the paperweight in his hand and thought of the sled, they are closely related. It will be instructive to look at the modest object—the scenario of the film refers to it as "one of those glass balls that can be bought in any souvenir shop in the world"—which shares with Rosebud the glory of being the fulcrum of love; and especially to compare it with Winston's paperweight.

4.

The two objects are internally different, though externally much alike: while there is nothing movable in Winston's glass, Kane's globe contains a miniature landscape and a supply of white particles in a clear bubble so that when you shake it you see a gentle snow flurry. The role of the two objects in the lives of their owners is, however, identical. Seen from a practical angle, they have none: they are singularly useless objects. Neither in Winston's case nor in Kane's do we hear that they ever weighed down any paper. Both owners acquire them at a turning point in their lives. Kane lifts his from the wreckage of his wife's apartment that he has just demolished—she has just left him. Winston buys his in the shop where his feet have carried him without his knowing why. But we know why: it is the moment when his search for the past has come to the point of no return. By his simple purchase he sells himself to his enemies, as in other days men had sold body and soul to The Enemy.

The chunk of glass has at first a hostile connotation, not only for Kane but also for Winston. Walking away from the store, he finds himself followed and presently thinks of using the weight to smash his pursuer's head.[12] So his relationship to Julia, the presumptive pursuer, starts under an ill omen. The end of both paperweights also mirrors their first appearances. Winston's is smashed in the moment of his arrest, that is, at the onset of his destruction. Kane's rolls from his hand at the moment of his death and breaks on the floor.

The similarity is striking enough to raise the suspicion that Orwell took the motif from Kane. The question is of some methodological interest, as an example of how coincidence sometimes frustrates research and how we are thrown back on intuition. When the film reached London, Orwell was film critic for *Time and Tide*. *Citizen Kane* was reviewed in the issue of October 18 by another contributor, Alan Dent. The question is moot whether Orwell ever even saw the film. In fairness we must mention a peculiar choice of a word in Orwell's description of the glass globe: the coral in it was "like a sugar rosebud from a cake."[13] Still, I am inclined to believe that Orwell formed his image of the paperweight independently. A paradox remains in any case, since it is difficult to imagine two men more dissimilar than Charles Foster Kane and Winston Smith. Yet each has his glass ball, and each loves it with an attachment beyond any reason.

Welles followed his inclination and the demands of his medium: let the viewer figure out what he sees. Orwell, a predominantly ideologically motivated writer (especially in his later works), was not the man to resist the temptation to elucidate his themes and symbols. After the thought of using the paperweight for slaying has left Winston, we read that it was that same glass which first gave him the suicidal idea to rent the room above the store.[14] He goes on to explain to Julia the value of the object's uselessness.[15] His fantasies about the glass globe as the vault of the universe follow, and finally the violent end. In the last part of the book, after we have seen the glass shattered, we do not hear of it any more.

5.

Two rosebuds do not a summer make, but there are many other glass paperweights in modern fiction, and it is surprising how often we find similar motifs and sometimes the same words that we hear from Winston Smith and Charles Foster Kane.

Kitty Foyle has a glass paperweight. In its center is a girl with a sled, around whom a gentle snow flurry can be produced, and she identifies with that caged but protected girl. She takes the paperweight with her as a souvenir when her parental household breaks up.[16]

The heroine of *All This and Heaven Too* reminisces to her lover about a paperweight she has seen: "It's as if you and I and all Paris were caught fast in a little round globe with the flakes going round and round like frozen stars."[17] He presently buys her a similar one in an expensive shop in the Rue de Rivoli (he is that sort of lover, and it is that sort of book). But he dies soon after, and her life in Paris comes to a tragic end. She brings "a few possessions" over to America and displays them on bureau and mantelpiece—all but the paperweight, "this souvenir of the Faubourg St. Honoré and a snowy New Year's Eve. That was too poignant a memento to be kept in sight...."[18]

The play *Cold Storage* is a dialogue between two cancer patients and a nurse. One of the patients, a Jewish refugee from Nazi Germany, remembers that at a stopover in Lisbon another refugee, who was to be deported—*i.e.*, who was to be delivered to death just as the speaker is now to face death—gave him a glass paperweight. He now feels guilty because he has lost it.[19]

The world and the life of the individual can be seen both in the glass ball and through it. The bold cinematic shots through the splintered glass in Citizen Kane have their counterparts in similar shots in Syberberg's *Our Hitler: A Film from Germany*. Mephistopheles in Richard Burton's *Doctor Faustus* shows Faustus the marvels he can bestow (Helena in her beauty, a cavalcade in its splendor) through a piece of crystal.

A bubble that looks very much like one of those glass balls can be seen in Hieronymus Bosch's celebrated painting, *The Garden of Earthly Delights*. A young man and a young woman, both naked— Adam and Eve?—are apparently ready to make love but not really to enjoy it. The "delights" in this garden generally leave a taste of ashes. Its alternative title, *The Garden of Lusts*, expresses this more clearly.

The content of such bubbles or globes is not limited to two persons. We have seen that they can contain the whole world. So it may be just one step from the glass globe that symbolizes its owner's refuge to the globe that represents the universe. This may be taken in two steps. The first step leads to those orbs that mock the idea that their owners can hold the world in their hands. The classical case is that of Charlie Chaplin as *The Great Dictator* (in the film of that name) dancing with a globe of the world until the balloon suddenly bursts. In Tolstoy's *War and Peace*, the portrait of Napoleon's young son, the King of Rome, showing him playing with a globe, was presumably made to make his father proud, but Tolstoy looks at it more like Chaplin.

When we examine these symbolic paperweights, we find them pleasant, often amusing, invariably harmless and innocuous. They seem suitable both as souvenirs and gifts. This is not true, however, in the stories where they are seen in relationship to human beings, as symbols of their predicaments. Far from talismans, they then seem harbingers of misfortune.

For example, the sinister element in a recent story is displaced into an antecedent: a girl has been raped, her attempt at abortion has been a humiliating fiasco, and she decides on suicide. But having laid out the pills, she falls asleep. Her father, a physician and toymaker, removes the pills and leaves his daughter with a comforting note plus "a small toy, a glass globe with a frozen skater inside. When you shook it the spell broke. The snowflakes tumbled, the bells tinkled, and the girl danced in bliss." The peculiar choice of words—frozen, spell broke, bliss—seems to make this special paperweight a symbol of the daughter's defloration.[20]

6.

Could these various globes, especially those of glass, reasonably be called fetishes? Does Winston's paperweight fall into this category? These questions are not easy to answer because the word fetish has a relatively complex semantic history, beset by hesitations and by attempts to hold back where connotations could lead to unwanted results.

The term was once a purely anthropological one. Primitive tribes believed that certain objects (fetishes) were the seat of supernatural powers; they therefore worshiped them. The West, however, has given the word a second meaning: "fetish" in the psychopathological sense has been used throughout this century. Lexicographers, however, were slow to accept this meaning. The famous eleventh edition of the *Encyclopaedia Britannica* (1911) does not recognize it, and neither does the *Oxford English Dictionary* of 1933. By 1968 the *Britannica* allowed that fetishism "may be defined as the necessity to use non-genital objects in order to achieve sexual gratification," and that it may occur in "normal premarital" situations, such as during "those stages of courtship" where the man (fetishism is considered limited to males) cannot get direct sexual gratification. The book does not say whether such a situation was typical of the 1960s. In any case, this is not the function of the glass globe for Winston. Obviously, other materials would be more suitable, so it does not help us much when the *Britannica* quotes Freud quoting Goethe, who let his Faust say to Mephistopheles, "Get me a handkerchief from her bosom, a garter of my love."

Webster's Third International Dictionary of the English Language (1970) comes closer to our paperweight by introducing a third meaning between the anthropological and the psychiatric, referring to such usages as "making a fetish of discipline" or "the fetish that birth and station presuppose innate superiority." *Webster's Third* calls such usages the "broad" form of the anthropological usage; but since we all would seem more akin to the psychological deviants in our midst than to some primitive tribes somewhere far away and possibly long ago, it might be more natural to think of this "broad" usage as a derivative of the psychopathological meaning of "fetishism." So we will draw the net of our definition wide enough to catch Kane and Winston. "Fetishism" in this sense, the psychological in contrast to both the anthropological and the psychiatric, is simply the phenomenon whereby an object (insignificant in itself) can come to have power and meaning over the emotional life of an individual.

How can this happen? The answer depends largely on the extent to which the stages of the object's "seizure of power" are visible or buried. Here it matters less what we can grasp than what those in whose souls the process takes place are conscious of. At least three different degrees of awareness are easily illustrated.

The first degree is the situation where everything is seen bathed in the light of consciousness, a very familiar scenario which occurs frequently in real life and often enough in literature. Here someone possesses an object which may have no material value, but has sentimental associations because of its connection with a loved person or with an event remembered with nostalgic pleasure. Whatever unconscious motives may lurk in the depths are submerged beneath sufficient conscious motivation to explain everything that must be explained.

Examples from literature include Desdemona's handkerchief in *Othello* and the sword that the Schlegel sisters receive from their father in E. M. Forster's *Howards End*. The handkerchief is crucial to *Othello*'s plot: Iago obtains it when it has been inadvertently dropped, makes it his prime tool in calumniating Desdemona, thus driving Othello into his murderous rage. Probably not all who are acquainted with the tragedy, however, are aware of the handkerchief's further significance: it is Desdemona's "first remembrance of the Moor," and this is why she "so loves the token" which Othello has "conjured her she would ever keep it" that she has taken to kissing it and talking to it. Othello had gotten it from his mother, to whom in turn it was given by an Egyptian sorceress. It has powerful magical properties. It would be tempting to analyze the dropping of the handkerchief as a "Freudian slip," but we must return to the image of the paperweight. We should note, however, that we have here one connection of "fetishism" in the psychological sense of the word to the older, anthropological sense, but this is mediated by Othello's African background, and Shakespeare was hardly a good guide in racial questions. We could do worse than turn to the intermediate stages represented by some of the magic rings so beloved by myth and folklore, and by the type of modern fantasy that follows their lead: Gyges's ring which makes its wearer invisible, the ring of the Nibelungs in the various versions of that saga, and, more recently, Tolkien's rings of power (in *The Lord of the Rings*) that give their bearers dominion over all life (until they are destroyed). All these are of gold. There is another connection with our paperweights in *Olympian Spring*, the great epic by the Swiss Nobel Prize-winner Carl Spitteler—a ring of glass. Its breaking signifies that the conflicts between the gods have become unmanageable, and that their rule is approaching its end.

Ben Jonson's *Song to Celia* (widely known by its first line, "Drink to me only with thine eyes") depicts a fetish rooted in physiology: the poet sends a wreath of roses to his love, she breathes on it, and it smells no longer of roses but of her. This poem, so modern in its ambivalence, is archaic in its emphasis on smell. To Swift, body odor would already be an execration. (It has often been noted that Orwell seems obsessed with bad smells.)

Kane was torn from his sled as a boy when he was violently separated from his mother. To what extent he identifies the sled with her may be questionable, but he certainly identifies it with the glass ball that falls from his hand, dying, when he utters his last word, "Rosebud." The snow flurries, produced by turning the glass around, undoubtedly remind him of the sled; and thus he remembers—he who has long ceased to be innocent—some of the innocent joys of his childhood. We can assume that he is conscious of this much, but we can surmise that he is unconscious of something even more important beyond it; namely, that the paperweight is to serve him like the Biblical balm, "to heal the sin-sick soul."

This is our second illustration, the one where the significance of the object that serves as fetish can be said to be half conscious and half unconscious. Winston represents the third type: the glass ball reminds him powerfully of the past, but he does not know any more which part of his past. The strongest propelling force within him, which in the end makes the catastrophe inevitable, is his striving for the reconquest of his past. For him his personal past and the past of the society in which he must live—*i.e.*, world history—are inextricably ensnared within each other. Neither woof nor warp of that tissue woven by fate will yield.

A truly interesting psychological question arises only to the extent to which the power of the "fetish" depends on unconscious factors. That extent is in our earlier examples very small, in the case of *Citizen Kane* partial, in Winston's case almost total. Different schools of psychology will answer differently. Adherents of Harry Stack Sullivan will hold that an earlier relationship to another person, later made unconscious by conflict, must be hidden behind such an object. Interpretation of the "fetish" would therefore depend on finding that person—not an easy task here, since neither *Citizen Kane* nor *1984* offer more than vague hints that there was such a person. The point may be made, however, that in both cases the function of the beloved object is not so much that of protecting its owner as of trying to heal the trauma of separation from the mother; but this is the trauma beyond healing, and the glass ball opens itself to receive its ward into its womb-like hull. Essentially the fetish remains powerless. Adherents of other schools of depth psychology will also think such a personal relationship, long since repressed into the unconcious, very probable, but will also imply that the proposition that it must have existed may be built more on dogma than on empirical findings. They will look for the latter and will not be altogether disappointed.

The most remarkable feature of Winston's feeling for his paperweight is, from this angle, that he visualizes it as a miniature world, with himself inside it; this obviously pleases him. Kane's paperweight offers an analogy, for the snow flurries in its interior take place in a landscape, the landscape centers on a house, and that easily suggests the presence of a boy with his sled. This also is undoubtedly pleasurable.

Winston fantasizes that he could get inside his lump of glass and be safe forever. "The paperweight was the room he was in, and the coral was Julia's life and his own, fixed in a sort of eternity at the heart of the crystal."[21] How could the reader help feeling that here the protective power of the womb is imprecated and is visualized as though surrounded by angelic glory? Many psychologists would find our question simple: the glass globe would be nothing but a symbol of the maternal body, expressing Winston's longing to return to his mother's womb, into that hollow sphere where peace rules, where no impulse can disturb, and where all dangers from without are banished. Any such explanation, however, must be hypothetical, because it is doubtful, says Melanie Klein, whether it is possible for any person to remember anything about his or her life before birth. Perhaps, some have said, people have only begun to remember their intrauterine experiences since they have been reading in popular works on psychology that they should be able to do so. Our doubts are not apt to be mitigated by the observation that the literature of the past hardly seems to contain any hint that in earlier generations anybody yearned for return to the womb.

7.

We are now in a better position to ask what Winston's glass globe represents. A fetish? An amulet? A symbol? Or does it partake of the attributes of all three?

The most conspicuous element in the relationship of Winston to his paperweight, the one shared by all the other paperweight owners we have encountered in fiction, is his intense and irrational attachment to the glass. Let us keep in mind that these objects are inherently useless. They also do not represent any material value. Although we are not told how much four dollars would be in terms of Winston's budget, the circumstances lead us to believe that it is an amount he could easily afford to lose. This is at least as true of the other owners: Kane especially is wealthy, so wealthy that he would not even notice the loss of such an object.

Their attitude is more comparable to that of collectors. Winston, of course, is not a collector; his living conditions would not permit it, and it is doubtful whether in the Oceania of *1984* there are any collectors. We might say that he would be a collector if he could, and we might thus add a feature to his character picture.

It is not without interest that in present-day America glass paperweights are highly collectible. There is, apparently unnoticed by the reading public at large, a good-sized literature on such objects (there are also curators of glass paperweights at some museums). The literature includes two types: technical treatises on their production, and catalogs, guidebooks for collectors, etc. Individual glass paperweights are sold at auction (mostly from the middle of the nineteenth century) for several thousand dollars.

Current production has taken different turns. The glass globes that Winston and Mr. Kane respectively owned are no longer available "in any souvenir shop in the world." There is the elaborate and expensive *mille fiori* type, where very colorful insets in floral patterns or bold swirls fill practically the entire glass; and there are those where shaking will produce snow flurries, but these are typically small and cheap, made of plastic rather than glass. Neither has that "rain water" quality that Winston prized, the depths that one can gaze into and be stimulated to revery. It is hard to imagine anyone deeply attached to such an object, as are the paperweight owners in the fiction we have reviewed. Every one of them kept his glass ball as the apple of his eye, except the refugee who lost it on his flight to America—and felt guilty about it for the rest of his life.

Winston's paperweight has some qualities of a talisman, as it has some of a fetish. Its possession is an evocation of protective maternal power. In contemplating it he finds calm and a feeling of being safe. But the feeling is utterly deceptive: maternal power cannot avert fate any more than other forces can. The cherished object is made of glass, and an outstanding quality of glass is that it breaks. Having accompanied its owner in life, it does so in death. Its breaking coincides with his.

This is the basic idea of "sympathetic magic." Its best-known example from primitive culture is the voodoo practice of sticking needles into the waxen image of a person to be killed. But wax would and does easily melt away even if no needles were stuck into it. The special mixture of durability and perishability that is required for symbolization of more complex thought finds its far better material expression in metal. The sword of steel, the ring of gold, remind the fleeting generations of man of both the possibility of durability and of their own vulnerability. It was a matter of technological development that glass could not play this role in an early era. As long as glass was treated as a type of jewel, its tendency to break could not be perceived as its outstanding characteristic. Only in recent centuries has the symbol of the breaking glass goblet (and now of the breaking glass paperweight) been used so convincingly.

Since glass now vies with metal as a literary or cinematic symbol, it has been much used to reflect human weaknesses and destinies, but also and preponderantly by truly "reflecting": by supplementing metal and partially taking its place in the one function that glass is particularly suited for, as a mirror. The glass that plays a role in Kane's and Winston's fates, though, is anything but a mirror. Far from reflecting a world, these globes are miniature worlds in themselves. Though worshipped like fetishes and preserved like talismans, they are entirely incapable of offering their owner any protection. Their world, the worlds that they represent rather than reflect, are in their entirety worlds of illusion. Their destruction symbolizes the destruction of the illusions of their owners, whose whole lives were built on nothing but illusions.

8.

In being destroyed, the paperweight fulfills its destiny. All that went before in the story was preparation for this supreme moment. It is so climactic that it warrants a closer look.

Winston, alert even to minor perils and perhaps sometimes exaggerating them in his imagination, has been blind to the real threat. He cannot help noticing that Mr. Charrington has no visible source of livelihood, but he hides from himself the obvious conclusion. Up to the point when Julia slips that note "I love you" into his hand he has worried about her following him, but he has never worried that Charrington might be what now he turns out to be.

The "iron voice" says "you are the dead." The engraving of the old church falls, uncovering the telescreen hidden behind it. Winston and Julia have "sprung apart." They are ordered to stand back to back, and wait for the Thought Police, who already are breaking into the house, truncheons and hobnailed boots ready. Winston knows that the rest of his life, which he will fervently want to be shortened, will consist of torture beyond his imagination.

> One thing alone mattered: to keep still, to keep still and not give them an excuse to hit you![22]

Or is it?

> There was another crash. Someone had picked up the glass paperweight from the table and smashed it to pieces on the hearthstone. The fragment of coral, a tiny crinkle of pink like a sugar rosebud from a cake, rolled across the mat. How small, thought Winston, how small it always was.[23]

So there is one other thing that matters. It is small, pink, normally enclosed. When laid open to sight, it turns out to be surprisingly small.

Many men, even men who are not psychologists, and many psychologists, even psychologists who are not men, know that there are males who fret about their penises being shamefully small. It does not matter much whether they seem small by objective comparison with others or just small in a particular man's feelings. For someone of Winston's type, who always feels inadequate, who is utterly surprised that a woman can declare her love for him, that feeling can be strong enough to intrude upon his feeling of standing at the verge of a fate much worse than death. It is not easy to think of any other possible explanation for Winston's emotions. Its intensity even seems to color Charrington's behavior:

> His eyes fell on the fragment of the glass paperweight.
> "Pick up those pieces," he said sharply.
> A man stooped to obey.[24]

Why "sharply"? Is the Thought Police bothered by the need to replace a $4 prop that may suddenly be needed to bait the next trap? Does Charrington now have human feelings? Does he put a sexual value on the fragment of coral? Or does he talk out of character for the simple reason that Orwell could not imagine anybody, be it a member of the Thought Police, remaining unmoved when something is destroyed that has represented a refuge, a life, a world?

Much could be and has been made of all this. The glass globe could, among other things, represent the womb. The idea of the womb as the classical place of enclosure and protection was not alien to Orwell. The protagonist of one of his earlier novels made it explicit:

> Under ground, under ground! Down in the safe soft womb of earth, where there is no...hope, fear, ambition, honor, duty—no duns of any kind. That was where he wished to be....He wanted to go down, deep down....[25]

It is true that the womb referred to in this passage is a metaphorical womb. But nobody would use the metaphor unless he wanted to make clear that he was speaking of Mother Earth. The phrase "the safe soft womb of earth" certifies that the user of these words was thinking of the mother when he was speaking of earth; if he was not so thinking, he could have easily found other ways to refer to the inside of the earth. But if the glass globe is (among other things) the mother's womb, and the piece of coral (among other things) a phallus, don't we have here a fulfillment in fantasy of the most primitive oedipal wish in its most brutal, hence most tabooed, form?

This is the moment when we must remember that it does not behoove us to spin our own associations onto the author or his literary characters. It is time to rise again from that mysterious world "underground" to a world of plainer daylight, without forgetting, however, what we have encountered "underground," and mindful of the fact that these observations may still serve us.

9.

There is a freshman seminar at Yale University, I have recently been told, at which virtually every student will draw attention to the problem of the paperweight in *1984*. This is remarkable, even taking into account that Yale freshmen may be smarter than other people. There is no accurate information on how other readers respond to what is written about the paperweight in *1984*. To gather such material reliably would require a sizable research establishment. Nobody has funded one, and it may be doubted whether it would be worthwhile to do so. Observations made without the stringency of a formal research project indicate that most readers miss the passages, or at least their significance, or forget about the paperweight long before they forget the more obviously important parts of the novel. Since, however, scrutiny of the passages involved demonstrates that the paperweight does play an important role, we must wonder how Orwell hid it so effectively and why he did so.

The Yale students are, of course, not the only ones who have paid attention to the baffling globe of glass. So have other critics. Alldritt gives an understanding summary of the paperweight, though he does not mention the strange comments on its destruction.[26] Crick, for whom it was less necessary even to notice the paperweight (his work is more of a biography than a study of Orwell's writings *per se*), nevertheless devotes some space to discussing the globe. After noting Orwell's determination, expressed in "Why I Write," to take pleasure in "solid objects and scraps of useless information," he notes that the special, useless "solid object" we are discussing was for Winston a "lifeline to the past" that Orwell gave him.[27]

These were professional readers of *1984*. To the ordinary reader, the paperweight may not as easily reveal itself—or rather, it would not reveal itself to anybody easily, but the professional reader smokes it out. The way Orwell hides it from the merely curious is simply the device of placing it in fragments between long passages that are of far more exciting content (for *1984* is really, on one level, a thriller; we shall consider this when we come to give some thought to the book's impact as a whole).

As to why Orwell would have hidden the very object that is perhaps the most meaningful single symbol in the book, the carrier of the protagonist's significant thoughts and ruminations, we can, happily, make some educated guesses. That small lump of glass had to carry so many burdens—as fetish, as failed amulet, as symbol of many things—that perhaps the burden of provoking the readers' thoughts should not be added. At the very least such thinking would destroy the soothing effect, so needed for temporary relief from the horror of the main action, which Winston's glass-induced fantasies offer.

The rest depends on the merit, if any, of our suggestions about the possible meanings of the glass globe. If there are indeed any meanings inherent in the glass ball, and not merely those carried to it by a reader spoiled by psychology, and if Orwell, however dimly, perhaps, recognized this, he would have good reason not to want to rub the reader's nose into these connections with the powers "underground." It would be as proper for him to keep these hidden as it is for a study of *1984* to try to bring them to light.

VI.

THE INQUISITOR

1.

On a summer day during some year in the sixteenth century after His birth, Jesus Christ returns to Earth: silently and inconspicuously He appears in the center of the old Spanish city of Seville. The people intuitively recognize Him, hail Him, worship Him, ask for blessing and miracles. He heals a blind man, He wakes a dead child to life. The Cardinal Inquisitor comes out of the cathedral, and has his guards arrest the uninvited visitor from higher spheres. At night he visits the prisoner in His cell and delivers a monologue setting forth why the Church is and must be devoted to undoing Christ's work: Jesus had come into the world to give men freedom, to seek their willing love. When the devil, the "dread and wise spirit," thrice tempted Him, He rebuffed him; He ought not to have done so. Now the Church must take its clues from Satan. Mankind is not capable of responding to Christ: too mean to grasp His message or to act on it, people need miracles, mystery, authority. Dispensing these abundantly, the Church ministers to their needs. Only the Church can relieve them of the burden of freedom and responsibility, make mankind happy by taming it into an ant-heap of billions of sinless children. Why has Jesus returned to disturb the great work that has proceeded for fifteen centuries in His name—even if it is the opposite of what He had preached and what He had died for? Billions would be obedient and happy, ruled over by an all-powerful clergy, an elite of a hundred thousand who would carry the burden of all mankind's guilt, who alone, as tragic figures, would be unhappy. So in the morning the Inquisitor will have Jesus indicted, convicted, and burned at the stake. The masses that were at His feet today will stoke the fires tomorrow.

Christ never says one word. At the end He gets up and presses a kiss on the Inquisitor's withered lips. The old man shudders down to the core of his being. He decides not to try the prisoner and releases Him with the injunction, "Go, and come no more...come not at all, never, never!" The prisoner steps out into the night. This is, in abridged form (in fact, pitifully oversimplified), the substance of Fyodor Dostoevsky's "Legend of the Grand Inquisitor," a "poem in prose" embedded in Book

V, Chapter V of *The Brothers Karamazov*. The legend is a semi-independent work—the centerpiece of the novel, yes, but almost equally impressive by itself. There are, in fact, several editions of the "Legend" published separately, one of them with an introduction by D. H. Lawrence. Lawrence admired the work, but not without reservations. He remarks that "the man who put those questions to Jesus could not possibly have been a Spanish Inquisitor." Why, he wonders, "did Dostoevsky drag in Inquisitors?" The question can be answered. Dostoevsky did not "drag in" his Inquisitor, he found him: in Friedrich Schiller's tragedy *Don Carlos*, written in 1787.

I am not speaking here of the ideas expressed by Dostoevsky so much as the basic situation of the story, which is an expression—one might say, a confession—of Dostoevsky's religious ideas, including his aversion to the Roman Catholic Church (enhanced, perhaps, by the almost hereditary antagonism between Russia and Poland), and his revulsion against the modernistic ideas he had championed in his youth.

An enormous amount of criticism has been written on the meaning of Dostoevsky's "Legend," including some fairly outlandish interpretations. Ellis Sandoz, for instance, wrote an entire book on the Grand Inquisitor (*Political Apocalypse*, 1971), discussing such problems as whether "paraclete" really ought to be an appellation of the Holy Ghost, as in Catholic liturgy, or something quite different; and the possible connection between John the Baptist and the Antichrist. Dostoevsky encourages such flights of fancy, for ambiguities are built into his piece. Unless there are clear indications to the contrary, readers tend to assume that the main character in a story represents, secondhand, the author's own views; but here we have two equal main characters, the Inquisitor and Jesus, with opposing views. In fact, we have the author's opinions third-hand, for he presents the Legend as a piece of fiction invented by Ivan Karamazov. And what Dostoevsky thought of Ivan is a complex question itself.

But whatever the ideas—and I shall return to them—the situation comes from Schiller. Dostoevsky was steeped in Schiller's works, especially *Don Carlos*. He mentioned in a letter to his brother Michael how as an adolescent he had read that very play with a friend, and how enthusiastic he was about "the magnificent, fiery *Don Carlos*." That same brother wrote the standard Russian translation of *Don Carlos*.

In Schiller's drama, Don Carlos rebels against his father, King Philip II of Spain. The king, uncertain what to do about it, seeks the Inquisitor's advice. Their dialogue culminates in this exchange:

> King: He is my only son. For whom have I gathered?
> Inquisitor: Better for putrefaction than for freedom.

The Inquisitor's reply is an epigram which Dostoevsky elaborates into a program. Furthermore, Dostoevsky's Inquisitor, like

Schiller's, is ninety years old. In Schiller he is blind, in Dostoevsky he sees all too much, but a trace of the original image is left: he has "sunken eyes, in which there is still a gleam of light." In both works, all fall to their knees as the Inquisitor passes by.

It would be convenient to point to some conclusive evidence, preferably a remark by Dostoevsky, that Schiller was one of his models. But it does not seem that he ever made such a remark, and even apart from the fact that he died within months after completing *The Brothers Karamazov*, it is simple to understand why he didn't: every educated Russian—a small, important group, the audience for which he wrote—would know it. Schiller (1759-1805), though very much out of fashion today, was throughout the nineteenth century one of Europe's most famous writers. Anyone writing today about Hamlet would hardly feel the need to explain that Shakespeare had also written a play on the subject. It will therefore not surprise us that Dostoevsky's notebooks for his great novel contain seven references to Schiller, but none of them to the "Grand Inquisitor."[1]

It is also quite possible that Dostoevsky was so imbued with Schiller's play that he was not even quite aware of where his story came from. Philip Rahv, a respected critic of Russian literature, has suggested two other nineteenth-century sources: a short story, "A Dream," by the German novelist Jean Paul Richter; and a poem, "Christ in the Vatican," by Victor Hugo. Dostoevsky may well have known both: he was a voracious reader, in the first half of his life preferring German literature, in the second half French. Both these works feature a return of Jesus and His confrontation with the Catholic Church; but they are confrontations in Rome, the natural place for them, not with the Roman church represented by a Spanish cardinal.

The whole issue of whether Dostoevsky derived his episode from Schiller may seem a pedantic quibble, but there is a more important (though less apparent) connection between the two works, about one of which Dostoevsky may indeed have been unaware. In *Don Carlos* the Inquisitor intervenes in a struggle between a father and his son: the play ends with the King handing Carlos over to the Inquisitor, presumably to be tried and executed (the historical Carlos died in prison under somewhat mysterious circumstances). In Dostoevsky, of course, the Inquisitor has no personal relation to the prisoner he talks to. But what is Dostoevsky's novel about? Old Fyodor Karamazov has been murdered—as it turns out, by his somewhat dimwitted illegitimate son, Smerdyakov. But he had three legitimate sons, too, and though none of them has murdered him, they all have often been tempted (their father is presented as a wholly unattractive character). His death overwhelms them in a tidal wave of guilt. The novel develops as a presentation of their responses. Dmitri is convicted and sent to Siberia; though innocent, he accepts his punishment as atonement for the sin of having wished his father's death. Ivan goes insane. Smerdyakov hangs himself. Alyosha immerses himself more deeply in ascetic Christianity. This is, of course, an oversimplified summary; but it should suggest how the Legend fits into the emotional framework.

We must keep in mind that *The Brothers Karamazov* is a very complex novel. No one character can be taken as the author's spokesman. The work's ambiguity is an integral element of its profundity. Of the four Karamazov brothers, it is clearly Alyosha whom Dostoevsky loves; but it is equally clear that Ivan is closer to a "portrait of the artist as a young man." His creation of these two characters, representing as it were the young man he thought he had been, and the young man he had wanted to be, can be understood if we consider Dostoevsky's life and writings as a whole. Dostoevsky was eighteen when his father was murdered by his discontented serfs. From all we know about Dostoevsky's relationship to his father, the idea was probably not altogether unfamiliar to him that an old man might be murdered by somebody other than his sons, but that his sons might feel ambivalent about their father's death. He may have mulled this over for half a century before writing about it.

As a fledgling writer in the late 1840s, Dostoevsky was associated with a group of young intellectuals who more or less considered themselves revolutionaries; in any case, the authorities considered them so. They were actually nothing more sinister than a reading circle which occasionally made some remarks that could be considered anti-Establishment. As might have been expected in Russia then (and it is questionable how much things have changed), there was a police agent in that small private circle. He reported what he heard and how he understood it, and the "conspirators" were tried and convicted of high treason. It was a time of tension; the Czar had just helped his neighbor the Emperor of Austria crush a rebellion in Hungary. Several members of the little group, including Dostoevsky himself, were sentenced to death. As they were lined up for execution, at the moment the officer was about to give the command to fire, a messenger appeared with the Czar's "pardon"—*i.e.*, an order commuting the sentence to lengthy imprisonment. The men were taken to Siberia. Such last-minute reprieves, incidentally, were a favorite trick of the Czar at that time.

Dostoevsky returned to European Russia in 1858, a changed man. The cruel prank played on him and his comrades had done its work superbly. For the rest of his life he believed firmly that Russia, led of course by the Czar and the Orthodox Church, was the country destined to save the world. He loathed the West and all it stood for. Such reversals of views are known to psychology as "identification with the aggressor." Dostoevsky's life here foreshadows the story of *1984*: Winston Smith, subjected to even more severe tortures than Dostoevsky had to suffer, ends up loving Big Brother, the actual or symbolic head of the government that has persecuted him. *1984* also has its inquisitor figure: we shall return to that later in this chapter.

It was difficult for Dostoevsky to reconcile his new ideological position with the facts of its inner contradictions. Perhaps for this reason the "Legend of the Grand Inquisitor" speaks with two voices, the voice of its titular hero and that of Jesus Christ; and it is not entirely clear on whose side the fictitious creator of the two characters, Ivan Karamazov, would be, or even whom Dostoevsky would in the end think was more nearly right or would prevail.

Dostoevsky wrote the novels on which his fame rests after his return from Siberia. Most of them, especially *Crime and Punishment* and *The Brothers Karamazov*, his last work (1880), focus on murder, though not necessarily murder of a father; and while he fashioned them almost as mystery stories in the popular sense of the word, in truth the mysteries they probe are those of the human soul.

The Brothers Karamazov, which does deal with the possibility of patricide, is widely considered his greatest work. Sigmund Freud, not a man easily impressed, called it "the most magnificent novel ever written," and the episode of the Grand Inquisitor, "one of the peaks of the literature of the world."

2.

Schiller was less preoccupied with murder than Dostoevsky was, but even more preoccupied with rebellion. His one great work, the *Ode to Joy*, used by Beethoven as the text of his *Ninth Symphony*, was written in 1785 during one of the few happy periods of his life. It differs in spirit from most of Schiller's works. His youthful conflicts had run their course, having found a voice in the exciting plays that established his fame. He had not yet entered upon his real adulthood, which was to be marked by his "classical" works, failing health, constant financial worries, and a growing sense of guilt, rationalized as the alleged incompatibility of sexual gratification and moral peace or achievement. The joy expressed in the *Ode to Joy* was the joy over the possibility, here taken as fulfilled, of reconciliation between son and father, between man and God. In his plays—and it was as a playwright that he was world famous—this reconciliation is at worst impossible, at best something to strive for. They are filled with raging conflict.

Their one outstanding theme is rebellion: of son against father, of subject against ruler, of all combinations of the two. They are infinite variations on the Oedipus complex, transferring its psychic energy from the limited arena of the family to the greater battlefields of history. Schiller devoted his enormous talents as playwright, moralist, and philosopher to the search for the boundary between the forbidden rebellion that is to be condemned, and the justified one that is to be glorified—between legitimacy and illegitimacy. He did not, like Dostoevsky, completely reverse his political and philosophical opinions, but he restrained them. We might say that Schiller's glorious "second period" was something that Dostoevsky missed because he spent the interval between youth and settled adulthood in Siberia. Orwell was not in Siberia, but his rebellion against the establishment was natural. He lived in a time and under circumstances that would have made a happy transitional period between adolescence and adulthood extremely difficult to attain.

To appreciate the political implications of Schiller's concern for legitimacy, we must not forget that Germany in his day consisted of literally hundreds of states that were, in theory, independent and sovereign. The larger ones, notably Prussia and Austria, actually were so; the smaller ones pretended to be. The rulers of many of them imitated the larger ones in splendor and outdid them in profligacy, obtaining money by exploiting their people with a ruthlessness that today is hard even to imagine. Young men were literally taken from their beds at night and from church on Sunday, and pressed into the army, sent to fight for other kings in exchange for money. There is a passage in Schiller's play *Intrigue and Love* which graphically describes how this impressment worked in practice:

> Yes, there were a few forward fellows who stepped out of ranks and asked the colonel for how much per ton our ruler sold human flesh. But our most gracious prince had the regiment drawn up in parade formation on the Town Square and had the ring leaders shot. As their brains splashed on the cobblestones, everybody shouted: "Hurray! To America!"

American history recalls such forced mercenaries as Hessians, from the Landgravate of Hesse, whose ruler, one of the most notorious of these petty princes, sold soldiers to England to fight against its rebellious colonies. But there were others like him. Each set great store by being called *Landesvater*, "Father of the Country." Their dominions were indeed small enough to allow each of them to interest himself in individual subjects, much to the subjects' chagrin, often treating them as uncouth, unruly children.

The Duke of Württemberg, Schiller's *Landesvater*, took a great personal interest in the gifted young man. He prescribed what Schiller was to study and was not to study. He was outraged when Schiller, disobeying orders, wrote *The Robbers*, a play about an unjustly oppressed young man who became a rebel and an outlaw; and forbade him to write for the theatre. With the example before him of other older writers already in prison, Schiller fled. The Duke's armed men were on duty at one of his glamorous parties, so the fugitive crossed the border without trouble. *Don Carlos* and the *Ode to Joy* followed, and later the plays of Schiller's third, "classical," period.

It is not rhetoric that makes a drama great. And a simpler plot generally makes a play better than a complicated one. Schiller's later works may on both counts be considered superior to *Don Carlos*. But his enthusiasm burns nowhere brighter, and the figure of the Inquisitor is his most condensed and powerful creation. So Dostoevsky took the figure and filtered it through the experiences of his life and his changed ideas. In reviving the great antagonist from the play that had so impressed him in his youth, he looked at it from the quite different viewpoint of his maturity. To Schiller, who had lived through petty tyranny, the Spanish Inquisition was greater and more wicked than anything he could readily imagine. Making its head the spokesman for enmity to freedom magnified that enmity, making it a worthy object of his hatred. To Dostoevsky, who had also experienced the tyranny of an empire, one as unrestrained as that of the sixteenth-century Church, the Spanish Inquisition could no longer serve just as an object of hatred. He exalted the Inquisitor into a being of almost superhuman grandeur and malignity. His ambivalent attitude toward this powerful authority figure—which probably accounts for the fascination it has held for generations of readers—no doubt also reflects his own ambivalent political and psychological impulses.

3.

Now that we have seen something about the antecedents of Dostoevsky's "Legend," what about its progeny? In the hundred years since Dostoevsky died, references to that novel and especially to the Legend have spread so wide that in recent times we encounter them in unexpected places. Monsignor Ivan Illich, a priest of Yugoslav descent, was called before the Sacred Congregation for the Doctrine of the Faith (an agency of the Roman Curia) and questioned by its head, Franjo Cardinal Seper, who happens to be also a Yugoslav. Mgr. Illich relates the end of the conversation as follows:

> We were speaking in Croatian and as the Cardinal led me to the door his last words to me were, "*Hadjite, hadjite, nemojte se cratiti!*"....It wasn't until I was going down the stairs from his office that it struck me that he was quoting from the Inquisitor's last words to the prisoner in Dostoevsky's story....

The piquancy of the incident lies in the fact that Cardinal Seper is in organizational terms the direct successor of Schiller's and Dostoevsky's Inquisitor, and he uses the words that were imputed to his predecessor by the institution's enemies. But there is no longer any question of burning at the stake. The Church has come a long way in the past four hundred years. The real heirs of the Inquisition today are the totalitarian political regimes that seek to control both the souls and the bodies of individual citizens.

As the cardinal quoted Dostoevsky, so it often happens nowadays that a phrase from *1984* or from *Animal Farm* is, often inadvertently, used in conversation. Whether, if "1984" ever comes, its regime would somehow be softened as the Sacred Congregation for the Doctrine of the Faith has softened after four hundred years, is another question. O'Brien's answer in the last chapter of *1984* is a resounding "No!," and Orwell seems to agree with him. But we are not forbidden to hope, as Orwell himself must have passionately hoped, that in this he was wrong.

But these developments were still in the womb of the future a century ago, and Dostoevsky's Russian Orthodoxy must have impeded his understanding of the Catholic Church as much as it must have spurred him to speak his mind about it. Admiration for the Legend should not blind us to the fact that neither the Inquisitor's character nor his situation requires him to make, so to speak, a full confession.

This very incongruity, however, is but additional proof of Dostoevsky's mastery: he presents the entire Legend as a figment of the imagination of Ivan Karamazov. The psychological need to make the speech is there, but it is presented as a need of Ivan, not of the figure of Ivan's creation. Ivan's need is clearly even more impressive if it leads him to let the character he invented make a speech that is beyond this character's proper motivation. Dostoevsky, after all, did not want to show us Ivan as a capable writer, but as a suffering human being. No such problem affects Winston Smith, whose theoretical pronouncements are too undeveloped to matter; but the question of whether the book attributed to Goldstein presents Orwell's opinion is indeed similar to the question concerning what extent Dostoevsky stands behind his characters.

That alone, however, would never have given the Legend its extraordinary impact, even when read apart from the novel in which it is embedded; and it would not explain the author's high emphasis upon it, echoed by so many critics. Dostoevsky clearly had another aim. The Inquisitor's eloquence and Christ's even more eloquent silence speak to the readers of the book, and through them Dostoevsky speaks to all mankind, presenting for their choice two powerfully formulated and diametrically opposed views of the world and of the nature and destiny of man. That he speaks to his readers with two voices, rather than one, indicates that he imagines Ivan as unable quite to make up his mind; but it also demonstrates how Dostoevsky himself follows the doctrine of Christ as he understands it, for in letting his Inquisitor sum up the teachings of Christ, he puts great stress on human freedom.

It is, however, but a secondary function of the Inquisitor to expound the teachings of Christ. His primary function is to reveal the philosophy which guides him and the institution that he dominates and represents. In creating the character of the Inquisitor largely for this function, Dostoevsky followed a traditional pattern which has long had a place in literature, and has maintained it even though it seldom occurs in a form that is convincing in realistic psychological terms—its usefulness has made up for its lack of realism. This pattern is that of the guide.

4.

The pattern of the guide is distinctly related to the motif of the Grand Inquisitor, though the relationship is so far from obvious that very little has been made of it by critics. The guide who explains to foreigners the inner workings of the country they visit occurred in literature long before Dostoevsky, but it acquired a new dimension when his Legend penetrated international awareness.

A guide naturally comes in handy in travelogues, but there the pattern usually is unobtrusive. As long as an author describes a country actually existing in the here and now, on this earth, we do not expect it to be so radically different that the traveller cannot draw his conclusions from what he sees. Works that present fictitious worlds or at least fictitious social or political systems offer a greater challenge.

This category, for which I like the generic name "heterotopia," comprises utopias (both eutopias and dystopias)[2] as well as many works of science fiction and fantasy. Heterotopias are written for the very purpose of showing an alien system, and, from the first, the form has included guides to explain the strange worlds being presented.

The lost sailors who are hospitably received on the island of Bensalem in Bacon's *New Atlantis* (written almost four centuries ago) are given only preliminary information, until at last their leader gets a formal lecture from one of the "Fathers" of "Salomon's House," the great research institute which is the distinguishing feature and in fact the very *raison d'être* of that happy commonwealth. Essentially similar lectures take place in Bellamy's *Looking Backward*, Herzl's *Old-New Land*, and even in such relatively recent works as Skinner's *Walden Two*, or, on a lower intellectual level, *This Perfect Day* by Ira Levin (also known as the author of *Rosemary's Baby*). Some of Wells's works fall into the same category, and Alldritt has rightly pointed out that Orwell follows Wells's pattern:

> *Nineteen Eighty-Four*...begins by presenting a human being...in a world that is to him and to the reader strange and inhuman. In Wells this world is remote...and the hero is transported thither...Winston Smith, it is true, is not conveyed to the world of 1984; he has grown to manhood in that society and is a native

> there. Nevertheless, though in that world, Winston Smith, we are asked to believe, is not of it.

The reader's reaction is clear:

> ...with the hero, he comes more and more to desire some explanation...in the scientific romance it is customary for this desire to be satisfied...the hero at last encounters some figure with power and information who explains the mystifying world to him. In this regard Winston's long conversations in the torture chamber with the Inner Party member O'Brien serve the same narrative purpose as, for instance, Pendrick's conversations with Dr. Moreau.[3]

Aldritt also reminds us that Orwell had shown himself very impressed by Wells's *The Sleeper Wakes.* Orwell wrote in an article, "Prophecies of Fascism,"[4]

> Everyone who has ever read *The Sleeper Wakes* remembers it. It is a vision of a glittering, sinister world in which society has hardened into a caste-system and the workers are permanently enslaved. It is also a world without purpose, in which the upper castes for whom the workers toil are completely soft, cynical and faithless.[5]

After reviewing *Brave New World* as an extreme vision of the same general type, Orwell goes on to say that no

> society of that kind would last more than a couple of generations, because a ruling class which thought primarily in terms of a "good time" would soon lose its vitality. A ruling class has got to have a strict morality, a quasi-religious belief in itself, a mystique.[6]

And so in *1984* the upper caste is far from soft.

The narrative trick of using a guide-explainer has been beautifully caricatured by Stephen Leacock in *Afternoons in Utopia.* The satire is well deserved because there is something basically not quite above-board about the device: the explanation that is given is not really meant for the listeners within the story, to whom it is ostensibly addressed, but rather for a wider audience outside it, its readers. The explainers, speaking on behalf of the author—over the heads of the other characters in the story—may be the highest officials of the fictitious nation, but in substance they are little more than tourist guides.

As such they have become dispensable. Heterotopic literature has increasingly flourished, and the reading public can be expected not to need as much guidance to strange worlds as it did formerly; the authors of such works have become bolder. Ursula K. Le Guin, for instance, in *The Dispossessed* (which she subtitled "An Ambiguous Utopia"—in this also, utopists have become bolder) does not explain her two invented planets to her readers on the planet Earth; she lets her story tell itself. The same holds true for innumerable space travel stories and much other science fiction and fantasy.

Where, on the other hand, the figure of the guide-explainer has been retained, it has also been heightened; it has unmistakably approached the more exalted level of the Inquisitor. What used to be a simple lecture to a respectful audience has tended to become interaction, an encounter of crucial importance for the work's characters, especially the leading character. Lectures are still given, but the most typical case now is a ruler's lecture to one subject, more likely than not with the subject's fate hanging in the balance, the situation prefigured in Dostoevsky's scene where the Grand Inquisitor lectures his prisoner.

There are two reasons for this development. One is simply a change in public tastes, in two divergent directions, but contributing to the same result: the modern reader is no longer satisfied with the travelogue type of utopia. The writer, and presumably his public, want psychological and sociological depth; they want, to use a popular term, three-dimensional characters. In this sense heterotopias may be said to have become more sophisticated. At the same time, readers nowadays prefer fast-paced stories; they have little patience for long-winded, interpolated expositions, and in this sense our taste has apparently become less sophisticated. The other reason is that dystopias have almost completely displaced eutopias in twentieth-century fiction (to discuss why this has happened would lead us too far afield); the government of a dystopia obviously has more to hide, and the more that is hidden the more difficult the job of explaining: it can no longer be left to some humdrum guide.

The way out of this dilemma in real life is quite different from its solution in literature: in actual practice, we do not hear of a member of the Moscow Politboro revealing to the masses the true aims of the Communist Party of the Soviet Union. But such a non-solution would be very unsatisfactory in fiction; so the power of explanation becomes vested in a person who represents the supreme power in the utopian state, just as the Inquisitor could be understood by Dostoevsky and his readers as representing the Roman Catholic Church.

This confrontation of power with its subject generally leads to a decision, albeit sometimes a harmless one, as when in *Lost Horizon* Father Perrault instructs Mr. Conway, the man he has picked to succeed him in the rule over Shangri-La. It is still reasonably harmless when World Controller Mustapha Mond explains his *Brave New World* to the "Savage" and to the two natives who have befriended him, though here the iron fist begins to show through the velvet glove. It has become anything but harmless in *1984*, when O'Brien, member of the Inner Party, discloses to Outer Party member Winston Smith what Ingsoc, the system of which the very name is a misuse and perversion of English Socialism, is in truth all about.

Both Aldous Huxley, author of *Brave New World*, and George Orwell, author of *1984*, were strongly influenced by "The Legend of the Grand Inquisitor," and were well aware of it. However, the difference in the way they made use of it is of greater significance than the similarity in the narrative device. Huxley's World Controller has disciplinary power over the men to whom he reveals the inner workings of his realms, but his yoke is gentle and he talks to them urbanely in an office with the trappings of civilization. Orwell's O'Brien discloses his secret to Winston while personally torturing him in the dungeons of the Thought Police, named, with horrid mockery, the "Ministry of Love."

More importantly, Mond follows a human and rational course: he wants his subjects to understand why they are being treated as they are, so that they can better cooperate in the measures he is going to take, which are in the last analysis for their own good. But O'Brien acts out of wanton cruelty: no rational purpose is served by his explaining the aim of the rulers' power, which is merely to perpetuate itself. He knows that the question has agitated his victim and that the answer will crush him.

Thirdly, and most important, Huxley still followed the ideology of Dostoevsky's Inquisitor; Orwell reverses it at the pivotal point. Huxley's World Controllers still seek the happiness, albeit a debased version, of their charges, just as the Inquisitor in *The Brothers Karamazov* had.[7] At least this is what both these rulers claim, and we are given no cogent reason to doubt their beliefs. O'Brien, however, along with the ruling group he represents, pretends nothing and believes in nothing. What he allows his victim is a glance into a gaping void, indistinguishable from the maw of Hell. His image of power is "a boot stamping on a human face—forever." The entire enormous apparatus of the state, the stupendous system of degradation and oppression, the never-resting engines of torture—they all have only this aim, nothing else.

5.

All of these systems with their various inquisitors, grand and smaller, still have one foundation in common. It is the idea, taken almost as an axiom, that the great mass of mankind is and must be ruled by an elite. Change is desirable only insofar as it might replace a bad with a good elite; but even the bad elite is considered evil merely because of the errors of its ways, rather than from any innate viciousness of the system. Before Orwell, the ruling elite was mostly depicted as a benevolent (though perhaps misguided) elite. But Orwell makes the system of elitism itself as malevolent as—and the word is here meant descriptively, not as an expletive—Hell. Democracy may not be Heaven, but it is at least the clear, direct opposite of this special hell.

As far as Dostoevsky found his Inquisitor's ideology offensive, it must have been on grounds other than its incompatibility with democracy: Dostoevsky knew little of democratic states and detested what he knew. In contrast, Orwell fought for democracy through his literary work and as a soldier in the Spanish Civil War. There is nothing ambiguous about his attitude toward O'Brien's ideology.

Considered as a work of literature, *The Brothers Karamazov* is universally held far superior to *1984*, and the ambiguity of Dostoevsky's novel is one reason. Scrutinized, however, for their value as expositions of political philosophy, where ambiguity becomes a defect rather than a virtue, the two works draw much more nearly even. Both seem to agree that as long as human beings have power over human beings, this is what the power structure will resemble. But they do not say that there always must be such a power. Orwell did not intend his picture of a horrible future as a prediction of what will happen, but as a warning against what could happen if we do not guard against it.

Dostoevsky opposes his Inquisitor, the protagonist of power, with Jesus Christ, the protagonist of love and freedom. A generation earlier, Marx had predicted that once the proletarian revolution—his secular equivalent of the Second Coming—had smashed the capitalist regime, the state would "wither away," and domination of men would yield to administration of things. No state has as yet shown any clear signs of withering away, but it should not be forgotten that this was Marx's expectation, based on his "scientific" theory. He rejected utopias for not having such a foundation. He was of course talking about eutopias. In his lifetime, and even by the time he died, a century ago, there were as yet few dystopias, and hardly any attention was paid to them. It is hard to say whether Marx would have seen in PseudoGoldstein a further development of his theory or a caricature of it. It is certain that Marx detested all inquisitors, in reality as well as in fiction (though he had no special interest in the latter).

6.

I have been tracing the motif of the Inquisitor in literature principally from two angles, the psychological and the political-philosophical; but in the consideration of specific works it appears that the two approaches are inseparable. The drive to write and the choice of the theme stem from the author's inner psychological processes; while the thoughts he expresses in his work, the positions he takes on the issues involved, are the result of interaction between inner forces and the historical conditions.

The psychological driving force of the Inquisitor motif is the father-son conflict. Various works that feature inquisitors sometimes show this conflict openly, sometimes as a thinly-veiled threat, but it is always there.

Schiller's Carlos is killed by his father's order, but the Inquisitor is almost as decisively involved: he is the even older man who persuades the King to kill his son. Carlos had to die for psychological as well as for ideological reasons. Marx said that the ideologists of a class cannot cross the lines in theory that are imposed by their class in reality. Schiller's work is a good example. Feudalism still held sway over Germany a century after the English Revolution, while the French Revolution was already in full swing. Having long outlived its usefulness, it was a particularly mean and backward feudalism. The German *bourgeoisie* and lower classes did not and could not rebel, and Schiller's rebels had to perish. The only exception is *Wilhelm Tell*, and there Schiller had the inspiring example of Switzerland before his eyes, the only true republic within his experience.

The motif of patricide pervades *The Brothers Karamazov*. Though it is not overtly the motif of the Legend, it dominates the background of the episode. Dostoevsky had suffered from the tyranny of an empire a hundred times more powerful than Schiller's *Landesvater*, and an empire that was now beginning to show signs of possibly being amenable to transformations. He could distill profound general principles from his own struggles in that very large arena, and could raise the Inquisitor to the heights of metaphysical significance. At the same time, he merged the motif with the originally quite different motif of the guide-explainer, a fusion which later writers have repeated. In psychological terms, his Inquisitor represents the image of the bad father, Christ that of the good father; in political terms, the Inquisitor a hostile empire, Christ what Dostoevsky hoped Russia might become.

Use of the motif by writers after Dostoevsky never reached that level again. Huxley and authors of similar dystopias toned the struggle down, brought it from a transcendent battle between Christ and Anti-Christ back down to Earth, but did not otherwise change it significantly. Orwell did.

Trilling is decidedly right when he points out that Huxley blazed no new trails:

> Aldous Huxley, in *Brave New World*, rigged out the welfare state of Ivan Karamazov's Grand Inquisitor in the knickknacks of modern science and amusement,

> and said what Dostoevsky and all the other critics of the utopian ideal had said before—that men might actually gain a life of security, adjustment and fun, but only at the cost of their spiritual freedom, which is to say, of their humanity.[8]

What Orwell did was something entirely different, and he knew it. He was, of course, acquainted with the figure of the Grand Inquisitor. In "Notes on the Way" (1940) he writes:

> It is as though in the space of ten years we had slid back to the Stone Age. Human types supposedly extinct for centuries, the dancing dervish, the robber chieftain, the Grand Inquisitor, have suddenly reappeared, not as inmates of lunatic asylums, but as the masters of the world.[9]

Several critics who have written about Orwell have pointed out how O'Brien resembles Dostoevsky's great figure. Crick says: "O'Bri-en is his Grand Inquisitor"; Alldritt makes the same point,[10] as does Arthur M. Schlesinger, Jr.[11] A slightly different tone is sounded by Brown: "The leaders of *1984* are philosophical descendants, not of the Grand Inquisitor, but rather of Shigalyov and Pjotr Verkhovensky in Dostoevsky's *The Possessed*."[12]

Orwell did not change the psychological substance of the motif: the relationship between Winston Smith and O'Brien can be understood as the relationship of a son to his punishing father. Orwell's great innovation was ideological: he had no more patience with the proposition that mankind must be ruled by an elite. His rebel still had to perish as Schiller's heroes and three of the four sons of old Karamazov had to perish. But Orwell gives no indication that he thinks this is the end of the battle, or that he considers it an immutable law of nature that the rebel must succumb. Far from acting as a self-fulfilling prophecy, his novel has had some effect as the warning he intended it to be.

This is as far as the development of the motif of the Inquisitor, from Schiller to Dostoevsky, and finally to Orwell, has gone. It is difficult to see where it might go beyond this point. Any new direction would doubtless reflect psychological and political stresses developing unnoticed in the undercurrents of our civilization. To break with tradition and enunciate some new element would require a new genius of the order of Schiller, Dostoevsky, or Orwell. It is in the very definition of genius and of the newness of the possible new element, that we cannot know whether such a person will come forward, or what he might bring to this well-worked theme.

VII.

TRUST AND BETRAYAL

1.

To place O'Brien in the progression of inquisitor figures in other literature sheds light on him, but it does not, of course, exhaust his role in *1984*. The significance of that role can only be comprehended by explaining the relationship between him and the protagonist of the novel, Winston Smith. It is, to put it mildly, a rather strange relationship.

The link of the inquisitors with their victims in works before Orwell's was essentially determined by the formers' official positions. The inquisitor crushes his victim because it is his job to do so. The guide-explainer reveals the workings of his strange country to his interlocutor, because this likewise is his job. Schiller's Grand Inquisitor is called in to advise the King: he does not even talk with Don Carlos. Dostoevsky's Grand Inquisitor notices Jesus and sees his duty—his action is not premeditated. The guide-revealers, from Bacon to Huxley, guide and reveal because this is their job. These men do not go out of their way to find their victims or listeners.

It is strange that O'Brien has had Winston under surveillance as long as he did. It is even stranger how Winston walks into O'Brien's long-set trap. "For seven years," O'Brien tells him, "I have watched over you." At least, this is what Winston thinks O'Brien tells him—it may actually be Winston's imagination. He has, after all, just told himself that O'Brien "was the tormentor, he was the protector, he was the inquisitor, he was the friend."[1] The reader does feel, however, that, although O'Brien may not have actually spoken in this instance, Winston reads his mind correctly.

These seven years may seem absurd to many readers of *1984*: O'Brien surely must have had other things to do. That he should have followed Winston Smith, an insignificant worm, for seven years sounds like a paranoiac delusion of the latter. And since Orwell must have had at least enough empathy for such a delusion to invent it, it supports the suspicion that Orwell himself was paranoid. It is noteworthy, though, that Schiller's Inquisitor protests to King Philip that by having the Marquis de Posa murdered, he had deprived the Church of its right to have Posa properly tried and burned at the stake, complaining that "there lies destroyed the work of many years." O'Brien, or whoever speaks in his voice, is merely more specific. Also, the very fact that O'Brien is willing to devote seven years of his valuable time to pursuing a nobody adds considerably to the novel's rising sense of doom, and to Smith's (and the reader's) awareness of the omnipotent inevitability of the power of the state.

So Schiller's Inquisitor acts rather like O'Brien, even though there is no indication that Schiller was paranoid. The world of his works is not, like that of Kafka or Orwell, a world of hostile powers persecuting equally hostile victims. The difference between the two is that Kafka projects his merciless picture of the world onto an existing environment which his contemporaries do not interpret in the same way, while Orwell projects his onto an environment especially created in the imagination for the very purpose of serving as a screen for these projections. In other words, Kafka seems to see the whole world as "Kafkaesque," Orwell only the world of *1984*. This may still be highly subjective, but Orwell can not be said to deviate far from the general consensus: those who in real life have come back from countries that are as close to Oceania in *1984* as is now possible have reported similar impressions.

In his same dialog with the King, the Inquisitor says that Posa's life "lay comprehended, from beginning to end, in the sacred registers of the Santa Casa" of the Inquisition. This passage has astounded my students. They had not thought that such records existed prior to the FBI and the CIA. These lucky young people have had no reason to think of the Gestapo or the B.P.U. It is possible, though, as we shall still have occasion to consider, that Orwell himself also underestimated the degree to which the institutions which support the state of Oceania in *1984* were preformed in the Spain of four hundred years ago, or at least imagined by Schiller two hundred years ago.

Thus, it is not as remarkable as it may at first have seemed that O'Brien goes to such lengths to trap Winston. But it is curious that the normally cautious Smith should seek out O'Brien now, and even more interesting how he goes about it. The steps that Winston takes in contacting O'Brien are especially crucial, because the relationship he thereby establishes is the most important—we may even say, the only important—interpersonal relationship in the entire novel. His relationships with the other characters are paltry by comparison, since Winston is the only fully drawn character in the book, and since his dealings with others lack any significant emotional depth. This is obvious so far as his colleagues and neighbors are concerned: of friends or family he has none. His relation to Julia, seemingly the one great exception, has, as we shall see, no resonance either. But his relationship to O'Brien does.

Winston's role can be characterized in two words: blind trust. We learn in the very first chapter of the novel how fascinated Winston is by O'Brien, and on what flimsy grounds he builds up his myth of O'Brien, the enemy of the Party:

> Winston had seen O'Brien perhaps a dozen times in as many years. He felt deeply drawn to him... because of a secretly held belief—or perhaps not even a belief, merely a hope—that O'Brien's political orthodoxy was not perfect. Something in his face suggested it irresistibly.[2]
>
> ...there was a fraction of a second when their eyes met, and for as long as it took to happen Winston knew—yes, *knew*—that O'Brien was thinking the same things as himself...That was all....[3]

Orwell knew that this was all, and that it was not enough, even though Winston did not know it. There was no other reason for him to italicize the "knew," except that Winston did not know and needed the emphasis to silence the warning inner voice which told him that to believe was not as good as to know. That voice could only be allowed to speak out when it was most clearly too late; when, after Winston's arrest, an unmasked O'Brien taunts him by saying that Winston knew it all along. Winston has no defense left and meekly admits it all to himself. But now the cruel interplay between Winston and O'Brien is merely beginning—its development is still in the mists of the future.

It is eventually O'Brien who takes the next step. Through a transparent trick he provides Winston with his address. Winston readily obeys what he thinks of as a summons to great things. He visits O'Brien. He takes Julia, by now his girl friend, along with him; but with one exception, which tells us much about her but little about Winston, she remains silent. She thus makes her own what he says:

> "We are enemies of the Party...we are thought-criminals...I tell you this because we want to put ourselves at your mercy. If you want us to incriminate ourselves in any other way, we are ready."[4]

Indeed, O'Brien does. He turns the dialog into an interrogation:

> "You are prepared to commit murder?...You are prepared to cheat, to forge, to blackmail, to corrupt the minds of children....to disseminate venereal diseases...If, for example, it would somehow serve our interests to throw sulphuric acid into a child's face—

> are you prepared to do that?...You are prepared to commit suicide if and when we order you to do so?"

Winston's unhesitating answer every time is Yes, while Julia says nothing till the last question of the series comes:

> "You are prepared, the two of you, to separate and never see one another again?"
>
> "No!" broke in Julia.[5]

It takes Winston a long time to join her in that No.

As the reader lets this sink in, he must not forget that Winston generally acts with the greatest caution and circumspection. He takes the greatest care to observe all the rules of conspiratorial behavior that people with anti-regime views have to learn under a totalitarian system if they want to survive—everywhere except where it matters. It is true that his trust in Julia is likewise blind, and his trust in Mr. Charrington equally so and as misplaced as his trust in O'Brien, but it is the latter which is deadly.

2.

Winston's behavior towards O'Brien is obviously very odd. It calls for some explanation, preferably one adducing some information about Orwell's own behavior or personality that would shed light on this oddity. Unfortunately, useful information about Orwell's life often just isn't available. In this instance, however, we are lucky: there was an episode in Orwell's life which reasonably parallels Winston's approach to O'Brien: his encounter with an Italian volunteer in the armed forces of the Spanish Republic. This fleeting encounter so impressed Orwell that he wrote about it twice: first in his book *Homage to Catalonia* (1937), and then in his essay "Looking Back on the Spanish War" (1943). There are some slight discrepancies between the two versions; *e.g.*, in the first, he says the encounter took place the day before he joined the Militia; and in the second, on the day itself. The description of the incident is the same in both reports.

The first report is at the very beginning of Orwell's book, thus setting its tone. He reports verbatim the oral exchange between himself and the Italian:

> The Italian raised his head and said quickly: "Italiano?"
>
> I answered in my bad Spanish: "No. Inglés. Y tú?"—

"Italiano."

These six words were all they exchanged. The powerful impression that the Italian made on Orwell was due to his appearance. Its strength puzzled Orwell himself, for he adds:

> Queer, the affection you can feel for a stranger! It was as though his spirit and mine had momentarily succeeded in bridging the gulf of language and tradition and meeting in utter intimacy. I hoped he liked me as well as I liked him....

Whether he did will probably never be known, for Orwell adds further:

> But I also know that to retain my first impression of him I must not see him again; and needless to say I never did see him again.[6]

Orwell did not, however, quite retain his first impression: he brooded over it and elaborated it. In his first report he guessed that the man "as likely as not was a Communist." By the time he wrote about him again, Orwell had become convinced that the Stalinists were the enemies of the people and that the Italian soldier "was probably a Trotskyite or an Anarchist":

> This man's face, which I only saw for a minute or two, remains with me as a sort of visual reminder of what the war was really about. It symbolizes for me the flower of the European working class[7] ....[and of] the struggle of the gradually awakening common people against the lords of property and their hired liars and bumsuckers.[8]

Orwell concludes his essay with a poem which he says he wrote two years later in memory of that Italian soldier, when the war was visibly lost and he was sure the Italian was dead:

> The Italian soldier shook my hand
> Beside the guard-room table;
> The strong hand and the subtle hand
> Whose palms were only able
>
> To meet within the sound of guns,
> But Oh! what peace I knew then
> In gazing on his battered face

Purer than any woman's!

For the flyblown words that make me spew
Still in his ears were holy,
And he was born knowing what I had learned
Out of books and slowly.

The treacherous guns had told their tale
And we both had bought it,
But my gold brick was made of gold—
Oh! who ever would have thought it?

Good luck go with you, Italian soldier!
But luck is not for the brave;
What would the world give back to you?
Always less than you gave.

Between the shadow and the ghost,
Between the white and the red,
Between the bullet and the lie,
Where would you hide your head?

For where is Manuel Gonzalez,
And where is Pedro Aguilar,
And where is Ramón Fenellosa?
The earthworms know where they are.

Your name and your deeds were forgotten
Before your bones were dry,
And the lie that slew you is buried
Under a deeper lie;

But the thing that I saw in your face
No power can disinherit:
No bomb that ever burst
Shatters the crystal spirit.[9]

It would not be useful here to attempt an evaluation of this poem. The essence of poetry, according to a famous definition, is "emotion recollected in tranquility." This, it can simply be said, Orwell's poem is not: it is raw emotion, recollected pugnaciously.

3.

We must remember that Orwell saw the Italian soldier's face for only a minute or two, and that they exchanged only a few words. Yet this sufficed to make Orwell rush headlong into utter intimacy, to feel the most extraordinary communion of spirits, and in time to develop this fleeting encounter into a symbol of overriding worth. It was the same overly ready willingness to trust that Winston Smith brought to his encounter with O'Brien.

How did this happen? There were significant differences between the two men, the real and the fictitious one, who evoked such a response. The Italian soldier was about as much below Orwell in the social and intellectual scale as O'Brien was above Winston. But their similarities were stronger, and these were in the area of general appearance and physical features. O'Brien had "a thick neck and a coarse, humorous, brutal face." Winston was "intrigued by the contrast between O'Brien's urbane manner and his prizefighter's physique."[10] The Italian soldier "was a tough-looking youth" with "powerful shoulders." His face was "the face of a man who would commit murder and throw away his life for a friend...There were both candor and ferocity in it,"[11] ...a "fierce, pathetic, innocent face."[12] It was clearly this type of face that attracted Orwell as the flame attracts the moth, and this was clearly why he fashioned his Winston Smith as a man to whom this face would have equal appeal. That the real flame barely seared, while the fictional flame burned to death, is the natural difference between reality and fiction.

What type of man would be so fatefully attracted to a comrade who combines muscle with a certain natural grace and charm with brutality? A man so drawn may be one who has suppressed homosexual leanings, but not with complete success: the leanings still motivate him, but he is no longer conscious of them. But plausible though this may be as a psychological theory in general, it is hardly applicable to Orwell. Nothing that we know of his life or find in his writings supports the idea. A homosexual who suppresses his tendencies is prone to a morbid sensibility in this area, an eager denial of any homosexual feelings in himself, combined with hatred and contempt against overt homosexuality. It is true that Orwell often referred to "nancy" or "pansy" intellectuals, but he used these epithets like many others he bestowed on those leftists whom he considered to be "worms" in the fruit of the movement to which he was committed.

There is one relevant episode in the autobiographical writings. One night he was locked up with a stranger in a house for vagrants.

> About midnight the other man began making homosexual attempts upon me—a nasty experience in a locked, pitchdark cell. He was a feeble creature and I could manage him easily, but of course it was impossible to go to sleep again. For the rest of the night we stayed awake, smoking and talking. The man told me

> the story of his life...Homosexuality is general among tramps of long standing, he said.[13]

Nobody who has trouble coping with his own homosexual feelings would be capable of this serenity.

The miners he saw in the North of England impressed Orwell differently. They were "splendid men," looking like "hammered iron statues," "nearly all of them have the most noble bodies," he relates after having seen them naked, though veiled in coal dust as in a tightly fitting garment.[14] He found it impossible to watch them at work "without feeling a pang of envy for their toughness."[15]

The word "envy" is the key word here. It's clear that Orwell's conscious desire was not to have sex with such men, but to be more like them to whom he was so humiliatingly inferior. If this is repressed homosexuality, it is that type of it which through sublimation has become ego-syntonic; that is, it has lost its capability of disturbing the harmonious working together of overt feelings and motives.

4.

We may start with Erikson's theory that trust or mistrust is established in infancy. We note that Orwell spent the first year and a half of his life as the youngest in an intact family. Then his mother took him and his older (and at that time only) sister to England. He hardly saw his father before the latter retired from his job in India and joined the family in England when his son was about eight years old, a point which he stresses repeatedly. He conveniently fails to mention a visit about the middle of that period, on which occasion his sister Avril, five years his junior, was conceived. At the time of the father's final return, the boy was sent to a boarding school, which he presently began to hate bitterly. He in effect had lost his mother as he had lost his father. The combination of all these events may well have led him to believe that his basic trust was bound to be rebuffed. He never unlearned the readiness to trust which he had acquired as a small child, but he learned to expect that it would not lead where he hoped it would. Thus it is not surprising that *1984* became a novel of betrayal. To go beyond such speculation, we would need knowledge that we simply do not have. It helps to know that the boy who was to become Orwell lived in England while his father worked in India. But we would need to know more.

There is a plethora of psychological studies about absent fathers and the effect of their absence on growing children. They cover a practically infinite variety of situations: the children of Norwegian seamen have been studied, as well as those of American soldiers in World War II. It has been explored how children develop when their father is in prison,

and what it means to be a boy if his father is a travelling salesman. The enormous range of situations makes it unavoidable that such findings differ widely. If the studies agree on one thing, it is that the situation in itself does not matter so much as how it is reflected in the child's mind, and that means largely how the mother's response to her husband's absence is transmitted to the child. We would want to know whether mail between England and India in the Blair family went once a week or once a year or not at all. Did father's photographs stand in a silver frame on the family mantel? Of things like these we know nothing. It is weak consolation that we would very much like to have such details about more consequential historic personalities, say Alexander the Great or Charlemagne, to say nothing of Jesus.

What is *1984* about? Considered as a political novel, as a dystopia, it is, of course, about malignant tyranny. Considered as a novel of interpersonal relations, it is about nothing so much as betrayal. Who in it does not betray and is not betrayed? Only the most innocent and the least innocent are exempt from the double curse, or at least we do not hear of them in quite this way. Parsons's children on the one end of the scale and O'Brien on the other betray with impunity. And only the most constricted and on the other hand the most open-hearted escape committing the typical sin; again, on the one end, Winston's colleagues are betrayed without themselves betraying, and at the other end the mothers do not betray. But consider the people in between! Winston, betrayed by O'Brien, betrays Julia, and she him. Nation betrays nation. The Party betrays everybody. And the only person whom we have come to know from the inside out, Winston Smith, betrays himself.

VIII.

THE SANCTITY OF THE WORD

What features of *1984* do most people find significant? What is popularly felt to be most "Orwellian"? Two things: the concept of Big Brother—*i.e.*, the feeling of one being always and everywhere under the surveillance of a stronger power from which it is impossible to escape. Secondly, the degradation of language. We may use a stronger word (which I hope to show is not inappropriate) and speak of the rape of language.

This had, of course, long been a preoccupation of Orwell, but it grew with time. The origin of such degradation was rooted in the self-perceived need of governments to present their horrible actions in a better light than they deserved. As Orwell wrote in 1944, at a time when he had become very bored with official and semi-official British propaganda:

> "We shall not sheathe the sword" sounds a lot more gentlemanly than "We will keep on dropping block-busters," though in effect it means the same.[1]

Orwell's denunciation of such practices reached a famous height in his description in *Animal Farm* of the pigs surreptitiously changing the long established and posted rules of the commonwealth. The climax is reached when the hallowed rule ALL ANIMALS ARE EQUAL is found to read

> ALL ANIMALS ARE EQUAL
> BUT SOME ANIMALS ARE MORE EQUAL THAN OTHERS[2]

Along with "Big Brother is watching you," this is the most condensed and therefore the most enduring formulation of what he found especially detestable. But at the very beginning of *1984*, just after we have been introduced to the ubiquitous picture of Big Brother, Orwell's condemnation of his regime is focused purely on language. Its cold tone enhances rather than masks its fire and fury:

> They were the homes of the four Ministries between which the entire apparatus of government was divided: the Ministry of Truth, which concerned itself with news, entertainment and education, and the fine arts; the Ministry of Peace, which concerned itself with war; the Ministry of Love, which maintained law and order; and the Ministry of Plenty, which was responsible for economic affairs.[3]

The ideology of the government that operates through these four ministries is called Ingsoc, a contraction of "English Socialism" and clearly the opposite of Socialism as the word has always been meant and understood. It is not very English, either, since England, having become a province of the superpower Oceania, has been renamed "Airstrip One." Furthermore, the ruling system of the two other superpowers, Eurasia and Eastasia, does not seem noticeably different from that of Oceania. The names of the ministries are at this point still given in English, albeit a perverted English, but their names in Newspeak (about which more anon) are also added.[4] We should also note here, to complete the picture, that the Ministry of Peace specializes in the massacre of prisoners of war; the Ministry of Love in the torture of political prisoners, ceaselessly performed in its huge white pyramid, which serves the same function as a tomb; the Ministry of Plenty in the issuance of periodic communiques announcing that certain rations have been raised, when in fact they have been cut; and the Ministry of Truth in lying (*i.e.*, propaganda and the deliberate distortion and alteration of history). Orwell has obviously described these ministries according to the maxim of Shakespeare's three witches, "Fair is foul, and foul is fair."[5] The four ministries manage with a high degree of success to "hover through the fog and filthy air."[6]

2.

But why pick out, of all the atrocities known to man, merely those against language? Why does Orwell speak of them, even more insistently than about torture and mass murder, as though they were the one unforgiveable sin? We must look for both historical and psychological reasons.

Historically, language becomes more important the more complex human society grows, the more the power of the rulers over their subjects is exerted by word rather than by direct overt act. This in turn is correlated to the development of organizations that increasingly take the place of individuals. Instead of man facing man, you have man facing an anonymous something where men are presumed to hide, but about the inner structure of which less and less can be asserted with any degree of certainty. You have what in modern English is called bureaucracy. It is a designation perhaps not entirely fair to the "bureau-crats," and we must keep in mind that its application is not limited to government. The process that has replaced the corner grocery store with the supermarket chain is part of it, as much as the process that once replaced the knight (who may, with his own sword, cut down a rebellious peasant) with the proud building from which orders flow to kill many men.

Here we must call on Longfellow's blacksmith once more to provide an example. Each age has its own horrors. The smith did not have insurance—if his smithy burned down, he was instantly destitute. But no agents hassled him, he did not have to negotiate with insurance companies, and in fact, there can have been but very few instances in the man's entire life when he had to deal with any man, except his minister, who was not merely a person of flesh and blood, but also the representative of an institution larger than any single man.

Things changed greatly over the next few generations, though not many people saw the change. That Franz Kafka did was the essence of his genius. It was perhaps easier for him than for many others, since he was a bureaucrat himself, working within the decaying Hapsburg Monarchy as an employee of the Workmen's Compensation Board for the Kingdom of Bohemia. His job was to rule on injured workers' claims for pensions. When Orwell wrote another generation later, things had become much clearer. He had but to project just one more generation ahead to reach the situation forever marked by the figure "1984." It is probable, however, that he underestimated the time that would be needed to change things so radically in the field of language, as well as in some other areas.

Both Kafka and Orwell were writers at heart, who knew from early life that they would be great writers, and who meanwhile spent their years in relatively humdrum careers in which they did not excel. Both died of tuberculosis in their forties. Both were unequalled masters in depicting the horrible—but not the horrible in the sense of the conventional horror story, where a force that is really outside common experience suddenly overwhelms the unsuspecting. Kafka and Orwell excelled in coming to grips with the horror that dwells in things themselves, that approaches inexorably without suspense. The protagonist (always much too miserable a figure to be called a hero) is always overwhelmed by fate, and must in the end realize that he had known of its inevitable triumph from the beginning, and that he has, in a sense, evoked it. Kafka's Castle and Orwell's Oceania are in some respects quite different social structures, but in this they are quite alike: Kafka's K. and Orwell's Smith deny to themselves that they know where they are going, but at the end of the road they have to admit that this was a pretext, that they knew it all along. This increases the pervading atmosphere of dread, but Kafka's repertory of weird and disquieting motifs was much larger than that.

All of Kafka's stories are set in worlds that are not quite our own, but this is true of different stories in different ways. The chilling effect of *Metamorphosis* springs largely from the fact that clearly impossible events are taking place in a most commonplace setting. *In the Penal Colony* is the other extreme of narrative structure: the story is set in a manifestly very foreign, very strange environment. It is the one Kafka story that most deserves to be called a utopia, and this would suffice to make it "Orwellian"; but it is, of course, even more akin to Orwell in its Regime, which is just as sophisticatedly cruel as that in *1984*.

Both Orwell and Kafka in their most characteristic work are mythical writers. The metamorphosis of Gregor Samsa into a gigantic insect (or whatever—Kafka made a point of leaving this open) is not only literally impossible, it is not symbolic either (*i.e.*, it does not stand for something else). Nor does it have any truly ascertainable meaning. Critics have sometimes denied this, not because it is unreasonable, but because it is so much against custom. (One of my students went so far as to challenge me to bring him scientific proof that a man could not be transformed overnight into an insect, just because it had never happened before. Anything is possible, he said. I replied that, while there is a rule that one must remove one's shoes before entering a mosque, there is no such rule obligating us to deposit our common sense in some cloak room before entering the temple of science.)

Every sensitive reader absorbs *Metamorphosis* with the unerring feeling that he has been allowed to perceive a deep truth. The same can be said to be true of Orwell, but somehow in his case this is not as easily perceived. The reason may be that in Kafka's works it is obvious that the deviations from our existing world are only introduced for the sake of the psychological problems that can be displayed against this background. *1984*, however, has all the trappings and reputation of an utopia, allowing the reader to suspect that the psychological complications are there for no other reason than to set his fictitious society against an even more gruesome background. It is of course possible that I overrate Orwell's psychological penetration, but I think the real reason lies elsewhere. His best-known works, those by which he has been judged and will be judged, *Animal Farm* and *1984*, are of a type where psychological depth is not expected; and not being expected, it is not found—one is a fable, and one is a myth, but both are utopias. The author of a utopia is expected to give his full attention to the elaboration of the social and political system he is describing; individuals are for him nothing more than the miniature figures of human beings in landscape painting, the millions of soldiers of which great warriors dispose, the proles in *1984*. Why should he then care about one of them?

Well, he does. It is known that writers of utopias often feel it a mere chore to describe people as well as institutions, and we can imagine that writers of psychological novels likewise find it a nuisance to describe *milieux*, when individuals are so much more interesting. Orwell's interests quite evidently spread over both.

Unfortunately, he knows perfectly well that Winston is in his own way a freak, that he can never achieve anything substantial, that he is essentially a "loser." Winston's own consciousness of these factors underlies his "mystical reverence"[7] for the woman who spends her days hanging up laundry (and singing); but she has "no mind."[8]

Winston's feelings about the washer woman probably reflect Orwell's feelings about the working class. He was better acquainted with the "underclass" of casual laborers, vagrants, etc., but in any case his attitude toward anybody below him in the social scale was a curious blend of near contempt and a feeling of inferiority leading to envy. It was undoubtedly colored by his perception of being (or at least believing himself to be) sterile. So the proles were the hope of the future, but not of an immediate future: first "strength would change into consciousness,"[9] which the proles in *1984* did not have, at least not to a degree worth anything.

Therein lies the significance of the psychological considerations we have explored, in addition to the historical ones, in understanding better the overriding importance of the question of language and its control. The starting point is easily defined by the problem of the consciousness of the masses that we just have touched upon. If people are to undertake the difficult job of preventing a regime like Ingsoc from coming to power, to say nothing of the much more formidable task of overthrowing it after it has become established, they must first be capable of thinking the thoughts that are needed to bring about a regime of freedom, peace, justice, and equality, and they must be free to think anything. So the rulers' natural wish is to restrict such thoughts and to eliminate any ideas that might be opposed to the ruling system. This can be done if thinking can itself be steered through language. Thinking *per se* escapes control; language, being overt, can be controlled. If we can only think as far as we can speak, then the intent of the oppressor can be fulfilled by limiting language.

But does thought depend on language? Is it true that we can only think what we can express in words? Orwell tended to believe so. This is not a new belief. It may well have originated in antiquity, from contemplating the difference between man and beast. Man is the only species of living beings that has the gift of articulate speech. And while we cannot claim that animals are completely incapable of thinking (or of communication), their intelligence is obviously a pitiful rudiment compared to ours. Nothing is more suggestive than the apparent correlation between these two observations, the uniqueness of human speech and of human intelligence. In the linguistics of the twentieth century the belief that thinking depends on language, that we can only think what we can put into words, is known as the Whorf Hypothesis, so named for Benjamin Lee Whorf, the scholar who gave the idea its modern form.

Orwell supported Whorf's ideas. He detested the depravation of language, not merely because of his "feeling strongly about prose style," but especially because such degradation also encouraged degradation of thinking. His accusation against the aging Tolstoy was that, in contrast to Shakespeare, "his main aim, in his later years, was to narrow the range of human consciousness. One's interests, one's points of attachment to the physical world and the day-to-day struggle must be as few and not as many as possible."[10] The "day-to-day struggle" was clearly the one that Orwell fought, with the typewriter at home, and with an old rifle in Spain. And the "attachment to the physical world" is the common denominator of the values that he proclaims as his in "Why I Write," and which seem there so oddly assorted: "to feel strongly about prose style, to love the surface of the earth, and to take pleasure in solid objects and scraps of useless information."[11]

It is interesting that the United States Supreme Court in a recent decision took a point of view rather similar to Orwell's:

> ...we have recognized that the State may not, consistently with the spirit of the First Amendment, contract the spectrum of available knowledge. In keeping with this principle, we have held that in a variety of contexts the Constitution protects the right to receive information and ideas.[12]

The court was responding to the practice of certain school boards of removing controversial books from school libraries. *1984* was not included in the case, but it is a frequent target of censors. One wonders whether such people actually wish to narrow the range of human consciousness, as Orwell put it, or to contract the spectrum of available knowledge, as the Supreme Court phrases it. It is not easy to think of any other reason why just this particular book should be thought to exert such a detrimental effect on the minds of students who often cannot even read.

It is impossible to overstate how much is at stake in the question of thought control through language control. When Winston and Julia muse that they will be tortured and will confess anything, they take comfort in the thought that "they can't get inside you,"[13] that "the inner heart, whose workings are mysterious even to yourself, remains impregnable."[14] If that last bastion falls, then it will be the regime that will be impregnable, forever.

If the Whorf Hypothesis is correct, then they *can* "get inside you"—not directly, but through language, if they can control and shape it. How else does one go about narrowing the range of human consciousness? Tolstoy had tried preaching and had obviously failed. The Spanish inquisitors had tried force: their murderous success was not as durable as Orwell wanted the regime of Oceania to appear. Its rulers must try something more sophisticated: keep people from thinking certain thoughts by making it impossible for them to do so. It is for this purpose that they have invented Newspeak to replace Oldspeak—*i.e.*, standard English:

> It was intended that when Newspeak had been adopted once and for all and Oldspeak forgotten, heretic thought—that is, a thought diverging from the principles of Ingsoc—should be literally unthinkable....[15]

But is that possible? The Whorf Hypothesis says that it is. Neither observation nor experiment can be easily arranged, so the hypothesis appears so far not to have been either definitely confirmed or refuted. It remains a hypothesis.

Orwell leaned toward it, evidently. If he had not, the whole invention of Newspeak would not have made much sense. On the other hand, he maintained a cautious attitude, so he ended the sentence that we just quoted a bit lamely: "...at least as far as this is dependent on words." Very well, but how far is that?

It is strange that the arguments popularly brought forth to support this theory merely prove the correlation between the variety of perception and the variety of names, but do not really show which of the two depends on the other. Eskimo languages have a large number of words for different types of snow. Languages in more temperate zones manage with just one. But ski resorts are never at a loss to describe the quality of their slopes.

The New York Times has raised the question: "what do you call the grass strip between the curb and the sidewalk?" In various parts of the country it is called a tree lawn, berm, median, park, or dog run. The paper adds:

> But for the most complete tribute to the Whorf Hypothesis one must look closer to home. There are few, if any, grassy strips between the curb and the sidewalk in Manhattan. What names do natives of the borough use for them? We asked several and they all said the same thing. They don't have one.[16]

It is hard to see how this should constitute a "tribute" to the Whorf Hypothesis. It shows, rather, that where something does not exist no name exists either, but that when the thing appears a name is promptly given to it. The procedure had seemed normal enough to Orwell in his pre-*1984* days. He wrote in 1940: "Aeroplanes and bicycles are invented, and we invent names for them, which is the natural thing to do."[17]

3.

To invent a new language, to force it on people, to actually replace English by that changeling, is one of the boldest endeavors that the ruling clique of Oceania would undertake. It seems a similarly bold and original invention on the part of Orwell. And in a sense it is. On the other hand, it is also true that he used the same method here that he used throughout his novel: he took something that he had observed in real life, extrapolated how it might develop within a generation, bent it in the direction of his political world picture, and out of these varicolored bits put together the mosaic of *1984*. The book's terrible clarity derives from the fact that so little of it is free invention, and so much of it direct experience.

One of the ideas that Orwell found alive in his environment between the wars was the idea of an artificially invented international language. There were several of these, to varying degrees artificial and international, only two of which had any significance: Esperanto and Basic English. Orwell was interested in both, at different times in his life, and he used elements from each to create Newspeak.

Newspeak is not, of course, an auxiliary tongue—*i.e.*, a language to be spoken only in communication with speakers of other native languages. It is, on the contrary, meant to replace standard English entirely. The need for communication with foreigners hardly exists in Oceania; in fact, the authorities want to eliminate such communication as much as possible. And the population has become so docile that this is possible to a degree formerly undreamed of. The real need of the rulers, in keeping with the Whorf Hypothesis, is to wean their subjects from their native speech, since English contains within itself a wide variety of ideas, a subversive thought in itself. Thus Newspeak must ultimately replace English.

Orwell was for a time interested in Esperanto; his favorite aunt (a sort of guardian angel in his Paris days), Nellie Limousin, was living with a man from Brittany, Eugene Adam, who was the founder of an international Esperanto association for laborers, and who was so enthusiastic about Esperanto that he did not willingly speak any other tongue. There does not seem to be any hard evidence that Orwell himself learned to speak, read, or write Esperanto, but it is very likely. A reasonable proficiency in Esperanto can be achieved in the proverbial ten easy lessons, by any intelligent and educated person who speaks one or more of the Western languages, and who understands their common structures and the fundamental ideas of grammar. Orwell's mother tongue was English, of course; he was also fluent in French, and had learned Latin and Greek. He says: "In my life I have learned seven foreign languages, including two dead ones, and out of those seven I retain only one, and that not brilliantly."[18] He deplored the wastefulness of this system and strongly advocated the use of an auxiliary language, but apparently never had a very positive attitude toward Esperanto.

He wrote an essay, "New Words," about 1940, although it was not published until after his death. He may not even have intended it for publication, but for a more limited circulation to stimulate interest in a "Society for the invention of new and subtler words." There he lets a hypothetical discussant say that "any made-up language must be characterless and lifeless—look at Esperanto, etc. The whole meaning of a word is its slowly acquired associations, etc."[19] The argument that he presents was quite probably his own, so this passage signals his switch from Esperanto to Basic English. His interest in this innovation grew with the progress of the War. In early 1944 he advised the readers of the *Tribune* (of which he was literary editor) to expect one or more articles on Basic English, explaining:

> If any language is ever adopted as a world-wide "second" language it is immensely unlikely that it will be a manufactured one, and of the existing natural ones English has much the best chance, though not necessarily in the Basic form. Public opinion is beginning to wake up to the need for an international language....[20]

This was written at a time when Great Britain was buoyed up by the proud feeling of having saved civilization, and when the American war effort was beginning to be felt. It has since become clear that the question of which natural language to adopt as an auxiliary was not just difficult, but so difficult that now it is the adoption of a natural language itself that must be seen as "immensely unlikely." Conversely, this does not mean that the adoption of a "manufactured" language has become likely. It may well mean that nothing will be done, and that our inability to solve this problem will be just one of those instances where we are unable to solve our problems intelligently.

By the time he wrote *1984* Orwell had come full circle. The artificial language was by now entirely evil, part of an elaborate system of oppression. Newspeak does indeed combine the innovation of going beyond the bounds of an auxiliary language with the disadvantages of both Basic English and Esperanto. Orwell was evidently bent on making it as unattractive as possible, heedless of thereby weakening the plausibility of his invention; for if a language is too ugly, it is less plausible that it could be foisted on the populace to supersede English. As it is, Newspeak has an English vocabulary, but its structure is taken from Esperanto; it is in fact identical with the latter in three important respects:

1. Simplification of words.

2. Complete regularity of grammar, especially verb forms.

3. Formation of words by adding, more freely than in any natural language, prefixes and suffixes. Hence such words as "doubleplusungood," and such verb forms as "I speak, I speaked, I have speaked."

Orwell invented these strange structures because he knew they would be repulsive to people. Just why they would be so repulsive may not be clear, but there can be little doubt that most people react to such linguistic capers either with hilarity or disgust.[21]

4.

Did Orwell go as far as anybody could with his idea of language as the force that determines the fate of civilizations? Not quite: there was an Austrian writer, Karl Kraus, who equalled or surpassed him.

A friend of his relates that he visited Kraus in 1931, at the time when the world was still reverberating with outrage over the Japanese bombing of Shanghai. He found Kraus pondering the proper positioning of a comma and expressed his amazement. "If the world had worried about commas in time," Kraus replied, "Shanghai would not have been bombed." Orwell would have understood.

Kraus and Orwell probably did not even know of each other. Kraus died in 1936, the year that Orwell really became Orwell. Their works were similar and dissimilar in some important and some unimportant respects. Kraus introduced his magazine *Die Fackel* (*The Torch*) with the hope that it would "shine on an empire over which the sun never rises": one would not expect an Englishman to write such a sentence. And one would not think an Austrian would write, "I hate mountains," as Orwell did.[22]

Kraus invented the documentary drama, and used it to heighten his meticulous mosaic of World War I into a picture of Hell no less infernal than Orwell's *1984*. Orwell wrote no plays, Kraus no novels or short stories. Both wrote poetry, to a lesser extent than prose. Orwell's verses were often poor, but he does not seem to have noticed. Kraus's verses were generally splendid, and he was perhaps only too conscious of it.

Their similarities appear in deeper layers. Both were journalists: their literary production was primarily stimulated by contemporary events and directed to influencing them. Both were polemical writers, not only by temperament, but because they saw so much more to blame in their worlds than to praise. History has shown them right. It did not mean that they were specially motivated by hate. On the contrary, compassion, in the true sense of the word (to suffer with), was the strongest motivation of both their writings.

It is hard to imagine either Kraus or Orwell as party men, though the latter went so far as to join the British Independent Labour Party on June 13, 1938,[23] characteristically at a late date for him, since it was long after the time he had wanted something of that Party (an entry into Spain in 1936). More importantly, in a famous letter to an American labor leader he declared himself explicitly "a supporter of the British Labour Party."[24] He wrote that letter to counteract the misinterpretation of *1984* as a defense of capitalism. It would not have occurred to him to write his novel any differently from what he actually wrote; he would have thought this dishonest; in old fashioned terms, he obeyed his daimon. The same was true of Kraus. Both attained their achievements outside of party.

Since they opposed things that were happening, both came to be regarded as revolutionaries, but both actually opposed innovations they considered pernicious, and were basically conservative.

They differed in physical size, and their life styles probably varied more than their different environments made unavoidable. Kraus, a Bohemian Jew, was rather short and not sufficiently well-endowed to realize his ambition to become an actor (his public readings were hailed as great theatrical experiences). Orwell was so tall that in group photographs with his fellow students at Eton, he immediately stands out. As a soldier in the Spanish Civil War he had to purchase his own shoes: the Republican government was not able to provide size 12 boots.

Kraus's favorite stance was that of the prophet shaken by divine wrath, the successor of Nathan, Isaiah, and Jeremiah; Orwell's attitude was that of the reasonable, normal man who speaks for common sense.

How normal and reasonable were they? Both Kraus and Orwell have been called paranoid. This would be of interest to us if it could be shown that this suspicion was based on similarities in the personality structures of the two men. But this is not the case. If Kraus gave people an impression of paranoia, it was because he had such a high opinion of himself that he thought of many events as specially significant for himself when they in fact were not. If Orwell gave any impression of paranoiac thinking, it was because he saw conspiracies where it was doubtful there were any. In Kraus's case, it would be megalomania if there was any clinically graspable phenomena; in Orwell's case, paranoia, if he had paranoiac ideas of persecution. We will discuss this further in Chapter X. Comparisons between Kraus and Orwell cannot enlighten us in every respect, but they can shed some additional light on Orwell's fascination with language.

The emotional preoccupations of Orwell and Kraus with language are evidently quite similar to the complex of feelings that we have already considered as fetishism. The main difference is that the "fetish" here is not a material object, like the globe of glass that serves or is pretended to serve as a paperweight, but an abstraction. The nature of the process becomes quite clear in some of the poems that Kraus wrote about language. Probably the most explicit of these states:

> With hungry heart and burning brain,
> Night after night I sought her.
> As a brazen whore I caught her,
> And made her a virgin again.[25]

The language of which Kraus speaks in this poem is the mother tongue. The term is not, of course, coincidental. Language is, in fact, closely connected with the mother. In Kraus's verses it is particularly the debased language that is identified with the fallen woman. The task of protecting language becomes the same as that of protecting the purity of a female idol. The fact that the language is the mother tongue helps to specify the female idol as a mother figure, since normally the mother is the first woman in a person's life to be loved and adored. The worship of the purity of the mother is the essence and the beauty of the cult of Mary in the Roman Catholic Church, as it has been in various other religions, although to certain pagan religions the figure of a fallen mother was not wholly alien.

The same complex of ideas played a considerable role in the psychological economy of Charles de Gaulle, a contemporary of Orwell whose historical stature and function were quite different. De Gaulle loved to talk about the honor, joy, and duty of defending France, the Mother. He knew that she was a fallen mother who needed redeeming, but he also knew that mentioning this fact would already be a breach of that redemption. Kraus could be more outspoken. Orwell did not connect his protective attitude to language with any problem of mother-son relationship. His silence makes it instructive to see how closely his work parallels that of Kraus. With the surfaces so similar, we have a right to speculate as to the underlying emotions of which Kraus writes, and on which Orwell says so little.

5.

The person who acquires a masterful knowledge of Newspeak cannot count on any reward or ceremony. He has the right to be proud, however, of becoming privy to a great and powerful secret, of partaking in an unusual mental achievement: doublethink.

The definition of "doublethink" is provided by Pseudo-Goldstein, but in the context it appears as authentic as if it were given by Orwell directly:

> Doublethink means the power of holding two contradictory beliefs in one's mind simultaneously, and accepting both of them...Doublethink lies at the very heart of Ingsoc, since the essential act of the Party is to use conscious deception while retaining the firmness of purpose that goes with complete honesty. To tell deliberate lies while genuinely believing in them, to forget any fact that has become inconvenient, and then, when it becomes necessary again, to draw it back from oblivion for just so long as it is needed, to deny the existence of objective reality and all the while to take account of the reality which one denies—all this is indisputably necessary.[26]

If we search in Orwell's literary past for some clue to the origins of Doublethink, we find some notes written in 1943 or 1944; Crick is uncertain whether they are "notes toward a story or whether they are simply autobiographical,"[27] but they sound like memories of Orwell's own, with himself thinly disguised by the initial B:

> Very early in life they believed that the doctor brought the baby with him in his black bag, but...learned that it had something to do with the man's and woman's sexual organs. They nevertheless had to rediscover this knowledge after having more or less possessed it and then passed through a period of ignorance. Thus at the age of six, B had played with the plumber's children up the road, until his mother found out and stopped him, and their play was largely sexual. They played at "doctors" and also at "mothers and fathers"...and both boys and girls inspected each other's sexual organs with great interest. Yet at about nine years of age he seemed to have forgotten all about it and had to have it explained to him by a school

> fellow... "You know those two balls you have—well, you know. Well, somehow one of them gets up into the woman's body, and then it grows into a baby." This remained the sum of B's knowledge for several years.[28]

The question of the authenticity of these memories is confirmed by noting a poem drafted by Orwell some years later:

> And the year was nineteen-nine.
> We played the games that all have played,
> Though most remember not,
> And the plumber's daughter, who might be seven,
> She showed me all she'd got....[29]

Anthony Panther West, whom we have previously encountered as a critic, was an illegitimate son of writers H. G. Wells and Rebecca West; he tells a story that shares with Orwell the feature that at one stage in life the knowledge of two contradictory facts flips into uncertainty of both:

> My father was quite a lot around when I was small, but I was never allowed to call him Father or Papa or Daddy. He was always H. G. But I knew what he was. And then by the time I was 5 or 6, I began not to know. And I became very anxious to clear up the point, because it struck me that I had only known intuitively—nobody had actually ever said it. So I asked my mother and she said "One day I'll tell you. There are reasons why I can't tell you now."— Anthony West, in an interview, January 1982.[30]

These phenomena are not restricted to such problems as sexual information or knowledge of paternity. In the lofty region of philosophical abstraction, which is the area of greatest interest to political systems which want to muddy the waters, similar conflicts between "knowing" and "unknowing" something are unavoidable. Theologians of various religions postulate an all-knowing and all-foreseeing God who has predestined everything, while at the same time telling their believers that every member must decide freely how to act. Not even the astuteness of highly intelligent and very learned saints has really cracked that paradox, any more than Job found a true answer to why God, being all-good and all-powerful, lets evil happen in the world.

These weighty considerations deal with more important subjects, but childhood memories show much more clearly how two opposing statements can be held true simultaneously, one representing forbidden knowledge. Doublethink is not so much an intellectual achievement as the result of an incompletely resolved emotional problem.

IX.

JULIA AND THE RATS

Fable and myth are often confused. In the world of facts, which is never as clearcut as the world of ideas, all sorts of mixed types flourish. Even though fable and myth are quite different things, at the very peak they may touch: some parables in the Gospels, for instance, may be considered as either of the two, or as an amalgam of both. But the normal fable is light, graceful, meaningful, civilized; while the normal myth is barbaric, rough, much older than civilization—it does not tell us that something has meaning, it tells us that something *is*. If we want to get the meaning of myth explicitly, we have to go to those later stages which interpret myth. If we want to hear a fable interpreted, that fable isn't worth interpretation.

When we read of the fox who could not reach the grapes and declared them too sour, we immediately understand both the meaning and the humor. We read of Saturn devouring his children: what does it mean? We learn of it as of a fact, but not really as one that at any time or place had actually occurred or could occur. The real world is hardly that extreme. The story of the fox, which has also not literally occurred, illustrates a human foible, and we smile. The practice of eating one's own children is not exactly what we would call a foible.

Myth stakes out the boundaries of behavior of which mankind may be capable. Just as the hyperbola keeps ever approaching its asymptote, but only reaches it in infinity, so the facts of the world approach myth without ever quite reaching it, but may be defined and understood by it. The truths of myths are primordial rocks—craggy, uncouth, naked. Their awesome shapes are not clothed in vegetation. They are anything but perfect works of art.

Animal Farm is a fable. It is the one work of Orwell's that by universal consensus can be called perfect—*i.e.*, as nearly flawless as any product of the human mind can be. *1984* is a myth: it is flawed. But its scope is greater; it is the more important work.

As so often in situations of this sort, the finding that *Animal Farm* is a fable and *1984* is a myth explains all or nothing. Answering the question of the nature of these two works has perhaps merely eliminated an object that had blocked the view of the next question: why did the same author choose to write a fable on the one hand, and a myth on the other? The difference in age and strength is one possible answer, for although only a few years separate *1984* from *Animal Farm*, Orwell had written *Animal Farm* while in tolerable health. It deteriorated fast. He had to finish *1984* in the hospital where tuberculosis had confined him. He never got home. Within half a year after *1984* was published, he was dead.

This is, of course, only part of the story. The themes of the two books are akin but far from identical. *Animal Farm* is clearly a satirical retelling of the Russian revolution. It ends with a state of affairs equivalent to the one that the Soviet Union had actually reached at the time Orwell wrote: stabilization, though on a level of internal tyranny, and externally a reasonable degree of acceptance by other powers. It is not relevant in this context that to the George Orwell who wrote *Animal Farm*, they appeared in many ways hardly less detestable than the object of the satire itself. The book does not attempt to predict the future. The reader can easily feel permitted to look at it with some optimism. After all, an even more vicious regime had just been vanquished, and euphoria may be considered the reader's right at least as much as the author's.

The situation a few years later, when Orwell wrote *1984*, was entirely different. The first disillusionment after the victory over the Nazis had set in. The spread of totalitarianism over the whole world began to seem no longer an absurd fantasy, but a real possibility.

The book predicts its invincibility. Curiously, *1984* can now be read in Mainland China, where the Chinese regime has settled on the comfortable theory that it is nothing much more or less than a satire on Stalinism. The text itself refutes this, but perhaps not so explicitly as to make it impossible to maintain that delusion. It is really a confusion of *Animal Farm* and *1984*. Of all the misunderstandings that have accrued around *1984*, this is still one of the mildest; but there is no denying that the two works, though informed by the same basic political spirit, are not by any means repetitious of one another.

When *Animal Farm* and *1984* are recognized as two fundamentally different works, *1984*—and especially certain parts of it—can be criticized in a sensible way as offering too stark a picture for even the most hardened readers. This is particularly true of the rat episode, which has often been called overly melodramatic, naively sadistic, and just not worthy of a writer of Orwell's stature. Even Orwell himself thought that he should have done better. It does not seem profitable to add to this debate, which in any case depends so much on individual taste, but I think it may be of value to turn to two more specific questions of psychological interest, and which are at least in principle answerable:

Why did Orwell use the rat torture? How was Winston able to divine what was demanded of him? True, O'Brien had hinted that if he wanted to save his own skin he had to betray Julia, but what clue or instinct can possibly have told him when and how to do it, and how did he know that the betrayal must consist of wishing on her the horror that he was unable to face himself, that only by this act would he snatch himself from the jaws of atrocious death?

There appears to be a fairly easy answer to the first question: in explaining to Winston his punishment, O'Brien remarks, "as didactically as ever," that it was "a common punishment in Imperial China."[1] But was it? Or rather, did Orwell have reason to believe it was? There is no direct indication that he knew or cared to find out, but there are two publications that he may have read which are only a little less directly pertinent.

One is Octave Mirbeau's novel *Torture Garden*,[2] a work that would clearly be called pornographic except for the fact that its stock in trade is cruelty rather than sex. Its simple plot places a jaded European lady on a guided tour of a Chinese park which contains some of the rarest and most gorgeous plants in the world, but is also filled with the most sophisticated and horrible instruments of torture. Torture is obviously practiced for no other purpose than the pleasure of the torturers, but this somewhat superficial similarity with *1984* can hardly have commended the work to Orwell. Be that as it may, the tourists in the garden encounter an old disgruntled employee who complains that he had invented a particularly "beautiful" type of torture which the authorities, however, failed to adopt—and he describes the rat torture.

Orwell lived in Paris in 1928 and 1929, for the avowed purpose of studying the seamy side of French culture. He may well have known about Mirbeau's book. However, as we shall presently see, it makes little difference.

A work which deserves much more serious consideration in this context, although it is unlikely that it served Orwell directly as a source, is one of Freud's classic case histories, "the Rat Man."[3] A reserve officer in the Austrian Army became a patient of Freud's after the following incident: while on maneuvers, he overheard a group of officers describe the rat torture as a punishment widely practiced in Imperial China.

Shengold[4] believes that the officer who described the torture must have read *The Torture Garden*. That would close the circle, as it were; but regardless of whether the officer paraphrased Mirbeau, described an actually practiced Chinese torture, followed a rumor, or made up the story himself, the effect on the Austrian was such that he consulted a psychiatrist. He was particularly upset about the connotation the story had for him. Freud reports that he could only relate it "with the greatest difficulty" and that

> his face took on a very strange, composite expression. I could only interpret it as one of *horror at pleasure of his own of which he himself was unaware*. He proceeded... "At that moment the idea flashed through my mind *that this was happening to a person who was very dear to me*." In answer to a direct question he said that

> it was not he himself who was carrying out the punishment, but that it was being carried out as it were impersonally. After a little prompting I learnt that the person to whom this "idea" of his related was the lady whom he admired.

If Freud had not heard the story from a patient, but had invented it after reading *1984*, he could not have laid bare the core of Winston's relationship to Julia any more tellingly.

Freud, of course, was long dead when *1984* was published. Whether Orwell knew Freud's work has not been established. It does not matter much, just as it is not important whether the rat torture was at one time common in China, or whether the story that Freud's patient heard had any basis in fact. It was obviously a well-established popular myth of its time, and Orwell can be presumed to have heard the tale related somewhere on his journeys.

One detail remains to be mentioned: in both Mirbeau and Freud, the rats are released on the buttocks of the fettered prisoner, they bore their way into his body through the anus, and he is eaten alive piecemeal from that end (although Mirbeau was not as explicit as Freud's patient). Orwell's rats begin by devouring the victim's face. Psychology calls this "displacement upward," but this bare designation does not tell us much. The likeliest explanation would seem to be that Orwell changed the story as he found it because he felt a need to: the frontal attack may have appeared just a shade less intolerable than the attack from the rear, as the latter is more suggestive of homosexual rape. And that may have been the one idea that made the whole story so intolerable to Orwell—that as he was trying to describe the ultimately insufferable, he still had to mitigate it to some extent, to civilize it, as it were.

Orwell leaves but one clue, a very ambiguous one: as Winston and Julia make love in the fateful room that he has rented for that purpose, she spies a rat. During the ensuing conversation, she tells Winston that there are areas in London where rats attack children. "'And the nasty thing is,' she adds, 'that the brutes always—' '*Don't go on*,' said Winston, with his eyes tightly shut."[5] The italics are Orwell's. As Winston learns when it is much too late, every one of their words has been recorded by the Thought Police, thereby providing O'Brien with the information he needs to develop the most effective plan of torture. Winston does not explain to Julia why he is so upset, but in his own mind he reviews a nightmare that he had experienced recurrently "thoughout his life." It involves a dark wall behind which there is something unendurable, the precise nature of which he knows and yet does not know[6]—a clear premonition of the climax of the great torture scene, when the rats will be revealed. But the reader has no inkling of this yet. All we know is that to Winston the rats are much worse than anything else he can imagine. From what we know about Winston and Julia, and from what we can guess about their image of rats, we can easily believe that Winston is here expressing his need—really Orwell's need—to mitigate the ultimate assault into a face-to-face attack.

All these are interesting questions, but they pale in significance before the much more central questions: how was it possible for Winston to betray Julia, so radically and so much in contrast with how he had been sure he would act? Had not the lovers promised one another they would never betray their love? Also, how could this act of betrayal ultimately have the effect of completely destroying his personality. To understand this, we must first understand Winston's love for Julia.

"Love" is a word with an almost infinite range of meanings, representing all sorts of relationships, usually with an added remark that defines it as a particular kind of love. But there is hardly anywhere, in literature or in life, a love quite as peculiar as that of Winston for Julia. The same does not hold in the opposite direction: Julia's love for Winston is relatively simple. A direct descendant of the cat in *Animal Farm*, she is not a character that revels in its complications. She seeks, and finds, sexual pleasure, spiced with the thrill of doing something forbidden, and of accumulating points in her game against the authorities she detests. This may even be the very reason why she is attracted to Winston, who is not described in the novel as the type of man who would normally be considered sexually attractive. We must remember, however, that our picture of Winston derives only from his own description of himself, and that in keeping with his character, this self-portrait may be much tinted to his disadvantage. We know that Orwell himself, based on the presumably accurate reports of others, was evidently much more attractive than he held himself to be.

Julia knows what she wants—and she gets it. Winston, however, "had disliked her from the very first moment he had seen her."[7] In the "Two Minutes Hate" soon afterwards, she stimulates sadistic fantasies in him that would not have been misplaced in Mirbeau:

> Vivid, beautiful hallucinations flashed through his mind. He would flog her to death with a rubber truncheon. He would tie her naked to a stake...he would ravish her and cut her throat at the moment of climax...He hated her because she was young and pretty and sexless, because he wanted to go to bed with her and would never do it....[8]

All this happens, of course, long before she, to his great surprise, declares her love for him. His dreams of her after the "Two Minutes Hate" are purely sexual,[9] but when he encounters her again (still having no notion about why she pursues him), he imagines bashing in her head.[10] When these initial obstacles are overcome, he is happy to learn that she has had scores, perhaps hundreds, of other lovers. And he sums up his feelings after successfully making love to her: "Their embrace had been a battle, the climax a victory. It was a blow struck against the Party. It was a political act."[11] This is not a very secure foundation for a long-term relationship; at the awesome moment when death very nearly does part them, they are far from seeking comfort in each other. Their first reaction when they hear the "iron voice" behind them say, "you are the dead," is different: "they sprang apart."[12] When Winston finally betrays Julia, he compromises little more than a former comrade in a campaign that has long since disappeared into defeat.

Winston's behavior—his total behavior, not merely his "love affair" and his "betrayal"—raise certain doubts: is such a performance plausible?

Intuition may provide an answer. My own subjective answer would be yes, but there is no way that science can answer the question rigorously. The science of psychology can determine through observation and experiment how people behave, but only to the extent to which observation and experiment are feasible; that is, within the framework of our world. Scientific psychology cannot predict what people would be like if a society like that depicted by Orwell should ever come to pass, any more than it can predict how extraterrestrials would appear, should we ever find any.

It is interesting, to note, however, that Shengold has presented clinical evidence to show that people of a certain type (with no violent impulses, but given to turning against themselves) will—in thought, if not in action—retaliate against "scapegoat objects."[13] In a footnote he makes clear that he considers the attitude of Winston Smith parallel to that of some patients in his practice. How applicable this is to reality must remain clouded by doubt.

The new world of *1984*, if it ever comes, will be inhabited by new men. But which will come first: the chicken of the new society, or the egg of the new men? Considered in the abstract, one answer may seem as likely as the other; taking history into account, it is clear that Orwell's *1984* could only arise out of the conflicts of our time, which are conflicts between our type of man. The new men must be the product of the new world. There is one outstanding trend in that new world: the trend to putting all love under the strongest taboo, except the love for the Party, the love for Big Brother.

So Winston is plausible. His "love affair" is the maximum private love possible between two individuals in *1984*, and even that is only possible as a revolutionary act, and must end in torture and death. Dostoevsky has presented the classical Russian conservative religious position that the inability to love is the essence of Hell. *1984* is hell: created by men, but not by its victims. It is not a creation of Orwell's fancy either, in the sense in which the stories about the Chinese rat torture can be called the fancies of those who spread them. Orwell formed his picture of what the world of *1984* could be like—would be like if we don't prevent it—

from untiring study of political developments that anybody could observe. But few had the intelligence and understanding that Orwell brought to the task; neither were they willing to take the risks he took.

The rat episode is indeed the most melodramatic and the most sadistic part of Orwell's last novel. It vibrates with the characteristic tune of the decline of our culture; it crawls with sadism because Orwell did not shrink from looking at sadism in its most developed and most detestable forms, at sadism victorious over humanity, and at sadism having become the overriding purpose of government.

X.

POWER AND PARANOIA

1.

We have in the preceding chapters given an occasional sidelong glance at the question of how power acquires legitimacy, how the holders of power convince themselves and the world that their power is theirs by right. Such diverse figures as Dostoevsky's Grand Inquisitor and Huxley's World Controllers derive their right to reign from their theory and conviction that their rule alone can make mankind happy.

The prevalence of this claim in pre-Orwellian utopism must not mislead us into thinking, however, that this type of justification was historically prevalent. Such claims flourished as a relatively brief intermediate stage between two more durable historical types. The feudal states never felt a need for justification in the modern sense. Power was dispensed through the grace of God, manifested in the state itself and in its rulers. The winner in battle won because the gods—later, God—favored him. Might was right before economic and social power began to shift from the aristocracy to the *bourgeoisie*, and subjects became citizens.

For reasons that would take us far beyond the confines of this book, the forces now assuming power had to do so in the garb of democratic ideology, deriving their rights, in the words of the Declaration of Independence, "from the consent of the governed."

The transition from the grace of God to the grace of the majority naturally took time. Various books, not just utopias, filled the interval with songs of praise for power (of whatever origin) used beneficently. How this concept underwent modification as the historic conditions changed can be shown in the works of two writers who critically accompanied the decline of the *bourgeoisie*: Henrik Ibsen and Thomas Mann.

In *Pretenders*, one of his earliest plays, Ibsen takes us into the heat of a civil war in medieval Norway. Heads of powerful noble families are fighting for the crown. Ibsen is clearly partisan: victory should not go, he makes clear, either to the man with the best pedigree or to the one with the greatest success; but he ought to be king who has "the kingly thought." In this case it is the thought that the crown should be more than enhancement of the power of the mightiest clan, that it ought to be the center around which the country is to be united and ruled, against the powerful clans if need be, and for the benefit of all the people. And in one of his last plays, *John Gabriel Borkman*, in a very modern setting, Ibsen still presents us with a concept of power that must and can be deserved and rewarded with power. Borkman, a banker, has financed his great enterprises by embezzling the bank deposits. When they collapse, he is sent to prison; after his release he plans his comeback:

> I wanted to have at my command all the sources of power in this country. All the wealth that lay hidden in the soil, and the rocks, and the forests, and the sea—I wanted to gather it all into my hands, to make myself master of it all, and to promote the well-being of many, many thousands.[1]

Asked in jest whether he wanted to awaken all the sleeping spirits of the mines, he eagerly affirms it in earnest. He virtually sells the woman he loves for control of a bank, because "the love of power is uncontrollable in me." And then there are the great steamships: "They weave a network of fellowship all around the world. They shed light and warmth over the souls of men in many thousands of homes. That was what I dreamed of doing."[2] He hears the factories working night and day, but even the woman who still loves him cannot hear the sound, because all he has left is hallucination. So ends the power of the *bourgeoisie* that in their great day thought they could make the wheels go round and make everyone prosperous and happy.

Mann wrote a parable of post-*bourgeois* power in his short story "Mario and the Magician." Here there is no concept of power benefitting the common weal, not even as hypocrisy, or hallucination. An uncannily gifted hypnotist bends his audience to his will. His show culminates in him convincing a young man that he, the hypnotist, is actually the girl whom the young man has unsuccessfully courted. He permits the man to kiss him. The young man is enchanted. After a brief, "evil span of time" in which Mario's lips meet Cipolla's "repul-sive flesh,"[3] the hypnotist releases his victim. The young man flings himself back, pummels himself with clenched fists, runs down from the platform, turns around and shoots the hypnotist. "An end of horror," the narrator remarks, "a fatal end. And yet a liberation—for I could not, and I cannot, but find it so!"[4] The reader understands that this parable is much enhanced by the fact that the story is set in Italy, at that time (1929) in the heyday of Fascism, and that it is fleshed out with details which let the Italian regime, then in power, appear both despicable and simultaneously ridiculous. If Il Duce did not reach the heights of totalitarianism, it was only because he lacked the resources or the imagination; he did not lack the evil intentions. The story was written almost twenty years before Orwell made the point that a totalitarian system would use sex in the service of the Party—"There will be no love except the love of Big Brother."[5] Mann's Cipolla is a forerunner if not a progenitor of Orwell's Big Brother.

In reviewing my material, I was pleased to find that Orwell's biographer, Crick, adduces "Mario and the Magician" in a similar context: after reporting that Orwell attended a meeting where the leader of the English Fascists, Sir Oswald Mosley, spoke, he remarks:

> ...from his perception of Hitler's and Mosley's mixture of sincerity and ability to bamboozle ordinary people, much as in Thomas Mann's parable of Fascism, "Mario and the Magician," sprang Orwell's own concern for truth, propaganda and the corruption of ordinary language.[6]

Mann did not believe, however, that the indubitable dignity of the *bourgeois* concept of power had inevitably to be so shamefully abandoned with the decline of the class that had given it currency. Attributing timelessness to its value, he ends his most extensive later work, his tetralogy of *Joseph and His Brethren*, with a great recognition scene that once again summarizes his idea of power. The Pharoah's mighty minister has revealed himself as the brother of the Hebrew refugees. He can enjoy having found them again, but they cannot. Will he not, so their conscience asks them, use his chance now to take his revenge on those who had thrown him into the pit and left him to die? They fall down before him and ask his forgiveness: "Repay us not according to your power." He will not even hear it:

> ...am I to use the might of Pharoah simply because I command it, to avenge myself for three days of discipline in the well and so make ill again what God has made good? I could laugh at the thought! For a man who uses power only because he has it, against right and reason, he is ridiculous. Or if he is not ridiculous today, he will be. And it is the future that we care about.[7]

To which Mann merely adds: "And so ends the beautiful story and God-invention of Joseph and his brothers."[8]

2.

Orwell understood that the old justification of *bourgeois* power could not be maintained, but he did not give it a humane and humanistic farewell, as Mann had done in the persona of Joseph. In *1984*, which in contrast to Mann's "beautiful story and God-invention" reads more like an invention of the devil, power is indeed used as a means to an end. It no longer seeks or needs self-justification.

The question may well be raised here whether, or under what circumstances, power needs justification. The answer differs depending on the nature of various theories of power.

Scientific psychology originated in the last decades of the nineteenth century. Theoreticians since then have largely limited themselves to attempting to understand the desire for power, the will to power, leaving it for later researchers to explore how power is maintained and why people tolerate it. Earlier theorists, among whom Machiavelli may be considered the most eminent, tended not to see a problem as later psychologists did; they assumed that it was natural for human beings to desire power.

One group of modern theorists who are still inclined to eschew research into the question of why humans strive for power are the ethnologists, who instead emphasize a quite different point. Konrad Lorenz, standard-bearer of the group, has speculated on the historic development of human aggression over the numerous centuries since man became man, but does not enter what he probably considers another province, the problem of the relationships of human drives to each other in the present. His principal point is that the continued existence of a species is safeguarded by nature in one of two ways: insofar animals are physically capable of killing or severely injuring other animals of about their own size, they are equipped with an inhibition against doing the same to fellow members of their own species. This has long been known: there is a classical Latin verse, *"Indica tigris agit rabida cum tigride pacem"* ("the Indian tiger keeps peace with the rabid tiger"). Where animals are not physically capable of killing conspecials, such an inhibition would be superfluous and natural selection has not favored it.

Homo sapiens is in a unique position. Having once belonged to the second category, he has now invented weapons (from the hand axe to the hydrogen bomb), which have radically changed this. Now man can kill man, but in contrast to other species where conspecials can be killed, man has no built-in inhibition against using his weapons against other men. Herein lies the irony and the peril of civilization.[9]

While ethnologists, like behaviorist psychologists, may consider the question of what role aggression plays in man as outside scientific study, or at least outside their own province of it, depth psychologists are not so modest. Or perhaps just not as aware of their limitations. The founder of one school, Alfred Adler, originator of "individual psychology," did indeed postulate in his early days that power was an overcompensation for a painfully felt inferiority, be it an existing physical inadequacy (Napoleon's extraordinarily small stature has always been used as an example), or the inferiority perceived by those downtrodden, oppressed, and discriminated against. Here the important fact is whether they feel that inferior; but of course, many men as short as Napoleon have not entered the arena of world history.

More is evidently involved. Freud, in developing the theories that were to form the great intellectual edifice of psychoanalysis, tried to cast a larger net and to catch more of the relevant material. The key word here is aggression. The desire for power is psychologically seen as one development of a more basic characteristic which consists of the readiness to attack other people, or in its wider sense other creatures or even objects. The drive for power can thus be seen as merely one form of aggression, to be elucidated with the wider phenomenon. Power is explained if aggression can be explained. But is it? There are still several possibilities. One can take a leaf out of Adler's book, as it were, and consider aggression a reactive behavior, a response to frustration.

In Freud's theoretical framework, frustration of the libido would come to the foreground, pushing existing or imposed inferiority into the background. Or, it is possible to take aggression as a given, in the sense in which ethnologists do so. Freud has enriched that branch of the theory by postulating a "death drive": that is, by assuming that there is a natural, universal, inborn drive toward death, toward decomposition of organic life, and in the interplay of the death drive and the sex drive (Eros and Thanatos with their mythological names), human life is played out. This is a controversial concept, as indeed it is bound to be, for it does not have the sanction that the other drives have in explaining actual phenomena. Inner drives are postulated where an action of the individual has to be explained and where that action is seen as necessary to keep a normal life going. Without the sex drive, there would be no procreation, the species would die out; without thirst and hunger, individuals would quickly die, with the same long-range effect. But dying normally takes place without any action on the part of the dying individual to bring it about, so how can one justify a death drive?

An idiosyncratic suggestion was made by Elias Canetti, who won the Nobel Prize in Literature in 1981, but he is not a professional psychologist. According to his view, man is forever faced, as his most difficult problem, with the problem of death. Man can neither imagine himself dead nor accept that he ever will be. His greatest desire is to avoid death, but this cannot be done in reality. It can be done in fantasy, however, by imagining oneself surviving as many other people as possible. Hence there is a strong desire to do just that:

> To be the last man to remain alive is the deepest urge of every real seeker after power. Such a man sends

> others to their death, and he diverts death on to them in order to be spared it himself. Not only is he totally indifferent to their deaths, everything in him urges him to bring them about. He is especially likely to resort to this expedient of mass death if his dominion over the living is challenged.[10]

Canetti sees herein the root of wars and heroes and hero worship.

A positive attitude toward heroism does not have to go as far as hero worship to be effective. Even a lesser degree of envy, identification, and emulation may suffice to give a ruling hero (*i.e.*, a ruler who has killed more people than other men have killed), a psychologically secure base of power.

Since we have never been told anything about Big Brother as a person, we have no way of knowing whether he has killed many persons, or even whether his subjects think he has. But the whole style of his power and of the power of the system that he embodies is certainly closer to the style of those African kings of precolonial times who throned on heaps of human skulls than to the power concepts of Mann or Ibsen. Marx and Engels have claimed that Socialism will follow Capitalism as a matter of historical necessity, but have mitigated the severity of that judgment by saying that historic necessity will be obeyed "under penalty of relapse into barbarism." As we look about us, what do we see?

3.

When we review the various concepts of power, we cannot help being struck by the fact that Orwell's is the most peculiar among them. It is easy to empathize with people who hold positions of power, or strive for such positions, if the power is of the nature depicted by Ibsen or Mann. It is, at least for the great majority of people, very difficult to have real empathy with a person who strives for a position of power, or holds it, where his aims are as entirely evil as those of Big Brother. What sort of person would fill such a position?

Orwell probably never had an answer to this question. This may well be why he waffles on the question of whether Big Brother actually exists, or whether he is some phantom of the Inner Party, invented to provide a focus around which the feelings of the subject masses can concentrate. When O'Brien says that Big Brother cannot die, we readily suspect that he cannot live either.

The fact that power in *1984* is so different from power known anywhere else raises a number of questions. First, how does it happen that the man and the position fit each other, at least outwardly, like hand and glove? This is a question which also has a far more general application: wherever in reality or in fiction we have a person fitting a position, or a position fitting a person, some explanation is in order. This becomes more difficult when we know little about how the person has obtained the position. In the case of Big Brother, we know next to nothing.

There are basically two possible answers, which I call the Darwinian and the Lamarckian. I do not mean to imply that any specific theories of Darwin or Lamarck respectively apply in either case; nor would I want to make a partisan choice in a field in which I lack expertise, between specific biological theories of those two scientists. There is little doubt, however, that in the decisive issue that divided them Darwin was right and Lamarck was wrong: evolution is not propelled by inheritance of acquired characteristics, but by natural selection between mutations and comparable differences which originate without regard to their adaptive value. The term "Darwinian" and "Lamarckian" as I propose to use them should merely designate styles of thinking on the problem of the mutual fit of person and position.

The Darwinian answer is that somehow among various persons the one who best fits the position is selected for it; the Lamarckian response, that the person being put into the position develops the qualities that make him fit for it. This style is exemplified by Lord Acton's famous dictum, "All power corrupts, and absolute power corrupts absolutely"; and the related nineteenth-century concept of the "Caesars' mania," the insanity Roman emperors allegedly acquired from the unrestrained power given them. Orwell does not assume either that the Party was corrupted by Big Brother or vice versa. Everything in *1984* is described as static. It is the very essence of the horror that Orwell's picture conveys that *1984* is a world in which there is never any change, in which everything will remain as it is, forever.

It is possible to see here Orwell's strength as a novelist, or rather as author of *1984*; his other works do not show such rigidity, neither do they possess its vitality nor its uncanny similarity to Hell.

1984 is a novel, so it is not the proper place for its author to express himself explicitly about his theories. The natural place for Orwell to do so was in the large body of essays he wrote, but even there we do not find much about his theory of power. The simple fact is that he was not a theorist. One expects a Michelangelo or a Rodin to form sculptures which perfectly reproduce the proportions found on living human forms; one does not necessarily expect them to tell you by how many inches the thigh is longer (or shorter?) than the leg, although it is also true that some of the very greatest (see Leonardo da Vinci) did both.

Few people would count Orwell among the very greatest theorists, and it is clear that his theoretical concepts are not always very well presented, or perhaps even very well thought through. This is as much true of his favorite positive concept, "decency," as it is of his favorite negative concept, "power." Others may have better described and analyzed the phenomenon, but there are few images as forceful and powerful in modern literature as Orwell's famous word picture of "a boot stamping on a human face—forever."[11]

We therefore will hardly be surprised, though we may well be regretful, that Orwell's theoretical writings do not show a systematic, well-designed exposition of power. We might be looking for a grand work, consistent in itself, and harmonious as a great achievement of architecture; what we find are occasional morsels:

> The central problem—how to prevent power from being abused—remains unsolved. Dickens, who had not the vision to see that private property is an obstructive nuisance, had the vision to see that. "If men would behave decently the world would be decent" is not such a platitude as it sounds.[12]

It is not a platitude, and it is doubtful whether anybody would think it is one, if only "decent" were defined operationally (so that the reader would know how to distinguish a decent action from one not decent); and if secondly we could be convinced that prevention of the misuse of power is truly the central problem. What if power is inherently the enemy of mankind, if, in other words, power is always and unavoidably misused? For an answer to this one we can again turn to one of Orwell's relatively early essays, but again we get hardly any comfort and not much more enlightenment: in a brief book review Orwell discusses the theory that every revolution leads to nothing more or less than the establishment of a new ruling class:

> The mass of the people never get the chance to bring their innate decency into the control of affairs, so that one is almost driven to the cynical thought that men are only decent when they are powerless.[13]

That comment was written in 1938, when Orwell was nearly ready to make his own the thought which he still called "cynical," and to face the question of whether the problem adumbrated by it was more suitable for a "Darwinian" or for a "Lamarckian" answer. Within a few years he was to begin *1984* and to complete that most important book within a decade after his wistful speculations about power. The "cynical" thought has become alleged fact: the decent are excluded from power. How has this happened? Did they turn indecent and gain power (the "Lamarckian" view)? Were they, as decent men, excluded from power (the "Darwinian" view)? We shall never be able to tell from studying *1984*, because this novel does not describe any rise to power or selection of powerholders; the power and those who hold it are described as though they had always been there and will never change. It is true that the Revolution which had brought it into being is mentioned, but only briefly and in schoolbook style—Orwell makes no effort to bring its story to life. For an imaginative picture of how power arises and how it develops the features that characterize it, we must turn to Orwell's other heterotopic work, *Animal Farm.*

4.

Animal species change, but not fast. A pig cannot become a chicken within the brief span of time covered by a short novel such as *Animal Farm.* The animal fable presents human characters in the guise of animal species. Within the novel they are immutable. This also eliminates the problem of sex between different members of the community. Here we have one reason for animal fables so easily becoming children's literature. The chance to downplay sex would have been welcome to Orwell, since, as many people who have considered the affair between Winston and Julia in *1984* have observed, love relationships were not his *forte.* In any event, the question of which grade in the hierarchy of power will be held by which character (disguised as species) does not admit either a "Darwinian" or a "Lamarckian" answer: everyone holds the place befitting the nature of the species. This was already so in the classical animal fable, but with one difference that is all-important. The classic fable was a moral fable. The various animals held the places in the hierarchy that befitted them. The man who is credited with having originated the type, Aesop, can hardly have believed in a personal, almighty, and just god, if he lived in the sixth century B.C., as is thought. But he must have been convinced of the rule of a just cosmic order. Later fablists ascribed this role to God.

Not a trace of that is left in Orwell's animal fable. The pigs rule because they are the fittest to rule; but this does not mean that they rule out of moral superiority—very far from it. The dogs tear the sheeps' throats out because they are trained for it and because it is their nature to be so trained; and the sheep have their throats torn out because this is the natural fate of sheep.

Since each animal acts according to its nature, there is no need in *Animal Farm* for any additional justification of power; and in *1984,* though we are here dealing with the interplay of the more malleable human characters rather than with the unchanging animal species, power is still distributed according to everybody's nature. It would be as hard to imagine Big Brother doing Winston's job as it would be to imagine Winston suddenly elevated to the top position of Oceania.

Having established this, we can shift our inquiry: instead of asking how Orwell thought that power was gained and maintained and how the person was fitted to the position, and vice versa, we can ask why he imagined Oceania as organized through a principle of natural fitness. The significance of this shift is greater than it appears at first glance. For it really entails the assumption that the society of *1984* is held together solely by negative factors: love plays no role, nor does personal interest; the only moving forces are hatred, fear, and hostility of all sorts. This is the world view of the paranoid. We must now ask: was Orwell paranoid?

5.

The arguments that have been used to show that Orwell was paranoid are simple. They derive firstly from the memories of the people who knew him. Two examples will suffice. Sir Richard Rees, who was one of Orwell's best friends and supporters, notes:

> Orwell was sardonic about the gradual relaxation of wartime restrictions. He professed that he had never believed that the blackout regulations would be withdrawn. Having once got us all neatly blacked out at night with no chinks of light showing, surely "They" would never allow us to show lighted windows again. He said, too, that he had not thrown away his ration book and clothing coupons because the apparent abolition of rationing must be some sort of trick.[14]

Isaac Deutscher, an anti-Stalinist Communist, author of biographies of Stalin and of Trotsky, wrote a quite critical and reasonably penetrating essay on *1984*, to which he appended these reminiscences:

> During the last war Orwell seemed attracted by the critical, then somewhat unusual, tenor of my commentaries on Russia which appeared in *The Economist*, *The Observer*, and *Tribune*. (Later we were both *The Observer*'s correspondents in Germany and occasionally shared a room in a press camp.) However, it took me little time to become aware of the differences of approach behind our seeming arrangement. I remember that I was taken aback by the stubbornness with which Orwell dwelt on "conspiracies," and that his political reasoning struck me as a Freudian sublimation of persecution mania. He was, for instance, unshakeably convinced that Stalin, Churchill, and Roosevelt consciously plotted to divide the world, and to divide it for good, among themselves, and to

> subjugate it in common. (I can trace the idea of Oceania, Eastasia, and Eurasia back to that time.)[15]

One wonders what Deutscher could find so very wrong with Orwell's view of the Yalta Conference as a "conspiracy," and one notes that Orwell recognized early—in fact, already as a schoolboy in World War I—that Great Britain was bound to drop out, exhausted, of the "Big League." This is carried to its logical conclusion in *1984*. We note further that the concept of the three superpowers has turned out closer to reality than many prognoses made by others. Deutscher's quaint description of Orwell's alleged shortcoming as "a Freudian sublimation of persecution mania," by which he seems to mean paranoia, shows Deutscher, not Orwell, out of his depth.

There are also a few remarks by Orwell himself that are somewhat of the same quality as those reported by others. In 1938 he thought that "what has happened to the freedom of the press in Italy and Germany...will happen here sooner or later."[16] He also thought that the concentration camp loomed ahead,[17] and as late as January 1939 he believed it "vitally necessary for those of us who intend to oppose the coming war to start organizing for illegal anti-war activities."[18] None of these seems very grave in itself, though, and while they may indicate defects of judgment, it is a long way from human error to psychopathology.

In order scrupulously not to omit any possible evidence for a paranoid streak in Orwell, we should also consider an incident that happened to him in the boarding school he hated.

> One day when I had been sent on an errand I went into a sweet shop a mile or more from the school and bought some chocolates. As I came out of the shop I saw on the opposite pavement a small sharp-faced man who seemed to be staring very hard at my school cap. Instantly a horrible fear went through me. There could be no doubt as to who the man was.[19]

The man was evidently a spy placed there by the headmaster! The latter must have served as model for Big Brother, and we can guess that the sweets the boy, Eric Blair, bought on the sly later inspired the chocolates the boy, Winston Smith, snatched from his sister. Such fleeting ideas of persecution would not be unusual for an insecure boy of twelve living under the pressure of a school which was its own miniature version of Hell, according to many accounts, not only Orwell's.[20] Reading what he writes about it as an adult, we almost see him shaking his head about such folly:

> It did not seem to me strange that the headmaster of a private school should dispose of an army of informers...I assumed that any adult inside the school or outside would collaborate voluntarily in preventing us from breaking the rules.[21]

There is hardly any need for arguments against the assumption that Orwell was paranoid. Surely the burden of proof lies on the other side. Even a man who holds unconventional opinions will hardly be called paranoid without some proof. And I have already commented on the weakness of those "proofs" that we have. We may add that in *1984* it is clearly the Party which deviates seriously from the perception of reality, as O'Brien's opinion about the stars demonstrates: "They are bits of fire a few kilometers away. We could reach them if we wanted to. Or we could blot them out."[22] Winston, though surely not wholly rational, is here the torchbearer of sanity.

Mann had in his exemplary story spoken of fascism as "something rather like an illness, perhaps..."[23] Orwell echoed this remark in 1946 when he said "that political behavior is largely non-rational, [and] the world is suffering from some kind of mental disease..."[24]

In contrast to the guardians of power, whom we may well regard as insane, Winston Smith suffers from a quite different feeling: a masochistic, self-destructive tendency that when mixed with the aggressive insanity of power forms an explosive mixture. O'Brien plays with Winston like a cat with a mouse. The essence of the "play" is that it is so rigorously choreographed. Anyone who has ever watched such "play" cannot help being fascinated by it. Smith and O'Brien merely reflect these roles. The play could not take place if the mouse did not act its part as prescribed, and O'Brien would be powerless to inflict harm on Winston if the latter did not do what he is supposed to do to help achieve the preordained effect. Winston's helpless compliance could almost be called morbid. Here Winston reflects the lifelong proclivities of his creator, as we have already seen.

6.

The worship of Big Brother, the longing to have someone to worship, has a double aspect, as do all important features of *1984*: a political-historical side and a psychological-moral side. From the political-historical angle, it is the desire for a great leader who will repeal the American, French, and Industrial Revolutions, who will undo what the last two hundred years of progress have accomplished, and who with his giant hands will push the cart of mankind back into the morass from which it came. Psychologically, the longing for Big Brother is the desire of the forlorn individual to find a lord and master who will direct his life in every respect, and who will crush him in the end. The image is that of a super-father, characterized by attributes once used to describe a heavenly rather than an earthly Lord. In an irreligious age such priorities must be reassigned. Like a God, Big Brother is both, inscrutable and all-powerful. Men who believe in God cannot presume to understand His intent; so also the subjects of Big Brother cannot presume to understand his actions or motivations, a mystique deliberately fostered by the members of the Inner Party. The present-day appeal of such cult figures as Jim Jones shows the vulnerability of certain personality types to this kind of influence.

Such feelings are not paranoid. Where shared by the culture of which the individual is a part, as in numerous historical monotheistic civilizations, including Judaism and Islam, there is no individual pathology. Where idolatry occurs as an individual feature not smoothly integrated into the surrounding culture, it is indicative of masochism rather than of paranoia. So if we are talking about Winston Smith, we can hardly find his attitude toward authority pathognomic. If we are speaking of Orwell, we cannot call him paranoid on the strength of his invention of Winston Smith. We may call him masochistic if we assume that the underlying structure is this: Orwell projected certain feelings that existed in his unconscious into the literary character he created. He could not permit himself to experience these feelings openly, as they were not supported by his culture, but he solved the dilemma by writing a novel. To make the feelings acceptable to the character, he invented the entire culture of Oceania so they would "blend into the woodwork."

Orwell also had to make Winston a much smaller man than he was himself. Canetti remarks: "If one is nothing oneself, there is a peculiar kind of servile gratification to be got from ending in the belly of power."[25]

XI.

THE END OF THE VOYAGE THROUGH HELL

1.

In summary, what might be called "the father figure as the Masochist forms it," Winston Smith's picture of the power that rules over him, is characterized by immense force and inscrutability. The power that will torture him until he is utterly broken stands before him like a blank wall. It can neither be climbed nor penetrated. It will never open or release its secrets. There can be no "Open, Sesame!"

We can thus formulate our principal hypothesis: *Orwell depicts the Ingsoc regime not as he thought it would be, but how he thought it would appear, filtered through Winston's mind.* It is an accepted principle of scientific procedure that a hypothesis can be tested by holding it against the established facts and seeing whether it fits— *i.e.*, whether it can explain the facts better than other hypotheses can. It must be discarded if it cannot. The hypothesis that passes the test will be considered promising and will be retained. In testing our hypothesis, this is what we find: some curious features of *1984* suddenly fall into place and become explainable.

The extraordinary speed with which the Party established itself becomes plausible, because this power is not to be measured against other yardsticks of history. Oceania is not subject to the limitations of other states. Its monolithic character becomes plausible because it is monolithic by definition, regardless of how much reality may mitigate against it actually being so. Winston cannot see it in any other way. Reading *1984* in an ordinary, unself-conscious way, we have the impression that the Inner Party is a small, coherent group. We may idly wonder about its hierarchical structure—*e.g.*, whether O'Brien outranks Charrington or vice versa. Only if we pay careful attention to Pseudo-Goldstein do we become aware, with bewilderment, that the Inner Party may have as many as six million members.[1] Reason tells us that it must have an inner structure, in fact a very complicated one, and that because of its large size and indubitably complex structure, the Inner Party will not be able to avoid conflicts within its own ranks. Indeed, the very text of *1984* tells us that members of the Inner Party are not necessarily secure in their privileged positions: Aaronson, Jones, and Rutherford fall from their heights into the lower depths of unpersonhood.[2]

Far from making the picture less probable, the inconsistencies in the account that Orwell gives of Inner Party workings make it more likely that this would be how Winston Smith would perceive it—without being subject to any streak of paranoia, but merely through the fact that his character is formed the way it is, and that his mind operates under the pressures that subjects of Ingsoc invariably have to bear.

2.

There are, however, some features of Winston's fate and of life in *1984* that our hypothesis can probably not explain, as, for example, the following: the sharp devaluation of sexual pleasure, which likens the sex act to an enema;[3] and the fact that some members of the Outer Party, such as Winston, though single, live in their own apartments (Julia lives in a dormitory, where surveillance by the Thought Police [and each other] is probably much more thorough). One would expect people to emancipate themselves from certain chronic shortages of goods through changes in their lifestyles—*e.g.*, growing beards instead of searching for razor blades. Perhaps the party forbids beards; on the other hand, the rulers of *1984* always try to make their yoke hard, but in such a way that it feels soft.

The extraordinary importance that a visit to a prostitute has in Winston's memory, with particular emphasis on her having "no teeth at all,"[4] is another such strange element, as is the catalogue of shortages and signs of decay.[5]

It would seem that our basic hypothesis cannot explain these things. We shall therefore need to introduce two subsidiary hypotheses: that Orwell injects into *1984* some features from his own London of 1948 (the shortages, the decay); and that he used such elements because they were a psychological burden on him which he could considerably lighten by putting them into a book. This would apply specifically to the prostitute, where the shock of seeing her toothless gums forms a rather close parallel to the petrifying (in the literal sense of the word) effect of seeing the head of the Medusa; the features that Freud in his notes on the head of the Medusa[6] singled out as psychologically relevant are clearly present.

Another item that belongs in this category is Winston's job and his attitude towards it. There is a rather striking contradiction between his passionate hatred of the Party and his serving it in a job at which he evidently works with great gusto. This reflects Orwell's ambivalence toward his wartime job of organizing propaganda broadcasts to Indian intellectuals for the BBC.

More importantly, it also reflects the difficulty of living in a country without contributing to its prestige and prosperity, and hence to the stability of the regime in power. The only ways of avoiding this are to "drop out," or to become a dismal failure professionally. Totalitarian regimes cut these avenues of escape. Withdrawal into private life is discouraged, and the tolerance for slackness in the job and for failure in general is much lower than in free countries.

If we examine those puzzles in *1984* that are solved by our basic hypothesis, and those which depend for solution on our subsidiary hypotheses, we find an interesting result: the features that form the essence of the plot in *1984*, as well as the essential features of the regime which rules Oceania, can all be explained by our first postulate. The subsidiary hypotheses are only needed to explain features which are of but secondary importance—while they contribute to making the atmosphere of *1984* unbreathable, they are not essential. If they were eliminated, the book would not collapse.

Let us note well that we are dealing only with hypotheses. Certainty is not granted to the critic. We must be satisfied with probabilties, but I think they can satisfy us. We do have enough to draw our final conclusions: Orwell was not diverted from straight political analysis by any psychopathology: his picture of *1984* is in substance derived from his clear view of societal developments around him, developments which he saw more clearly than did most of his compatriots.

He did, however, present his vision of the possible future in a manner different from that of the political scientist: he created the figure of Winston Smith as the man he himself would have been had he lived under the regime of Ingsoc; and he invented an environment to go with that character. To that extent his picture is distorted. The distortion is enhanced by his giving, in some instances, some features of the London of 1948 to its sister of 1984; and by inserting some elements, such as Winston's visit to the prostitute, that do not shed additional light on the main theme but merely represent Orwell's feelings on a problem that happened to be of concern to him. We can now breathe more freely; *1984* does indeed give a picture of a possible future which is somewhat affected by "hangups" of its author. Our future will not be quite so much like Hell as the novel makes us believe and fear. The horror as depicted may yet befall us, but it is not inevitable. We now have the reassurance that we were looking for when we began. We can terminate our tour through Hell with Dante's sigh of relief: *"E quindi uscimmo a riveder le stelle*"—"thence we emerged, to see again the stars."

3.

It remains for us to review, very briefly, the impact of Orwell's novel, which seems on the surface hopelessly unattractive. Why would anybody want to read of such horrors? There are indeed people who take this attitude: these may be facts, even important facts, but they are unpleasant facts, and the less I hear about them the better off I am. The book has nevertheless been an undeniably great success, an international bestseller, one of the best-known and presumably most influential works of fiction in our age.

On second thought, this appears unsurprising. *1984* is a thriller, and thrillers and horror stories have always exerted a very marked attraction, though only on certain parts of the reading public. It cannot be our purpose here to examine the psychological foundations of such attraction.

1984 is in any event not an ordinary thriller. It owes much of its effectiveness to the fact that it speaks a powerful truth. However, the unvarnished truth does not always attract. So perhaps the very fact that the truth is here to some degree distorted has actually helped increase the book's impact.

In this second half of the twentieth century, some of us have the feeling that we are living in a world over which we have no control, and which we can not even hope to understand. This situation predisposes many to paranoid thinking. It may be that *1984* has just enough of a paranoid tinge to accomodate this tendency, to strike a chord that many readers have half heard and have half longed to hear. In any case, *1984* has been able to catch the readers' imagination, and to lead it into channels it had prepared.

This book has also been the single most important influence in a combination of influences that disenthralled the Leftist movement in the West from Russia. After 1917 there was a strong tendency in the European and American Left to look to Moscow as the new Heavenly Jerusalem. This dependence not only largely cancelled out any impact that the Left might have had on events, it did not really help Russia, and it greatly damaged the cause of liberty and justice all through the world. To take Orwell's line, the line of uncompromising hostility against totalitarianism in whatever guise it appears, has been a real liberation.

Having thus helped to free us, this effort has improved our chances. It has not, alas, prevented the rule, in large parts of the world, of regimes almost as vicious on occasion as that depicted in *1984*. We can hear the screams of the victims in their torture chambers, and can do very little about them. This feeling of guilt is not the self-torture that Orwell himself so often felt. It is unreasonable only because the one thing that could radically help these people is the one thing that we cannot do: we cannot call for a sacred war of liberation. This would have been the thing to do in the past, but since the invention of the atomic bomb such a call would inevitably lead to the extermination of mankind, perhaps of all life on Earth.

We hope in the future somehow to wear down the enemy, and perhaps the collapse of communism in Eastern Europe is a sign of hope for the future, although many harsh regimes remain. But for now all we can give the victims of totalitarianism is our sympathy and a share in our hope. To those whose faces are being stamped on by boots, forever, our admiring and humble greetings.

NOTES

Introduction

1. Orwell, George. *The Collected Essays, Journalism and Letters of George Orwell*, edited by Sonia Orwell and Ian Angus. New York and London: A Harvest/HBJ Book, Harcourt Brace Jovanovich, 1968, Vol. 2, p. 266. This collection will be hereinafter cited as *CEJL*. As to the Italian soldier mentioned in the text, we'll have occasion to discuss him in Section 2 of Chapter VII. The "present war" referred to by Orwell was World War II.
2. Orwell, George. "Charles Dickens," in *CEJL*, Vol. 1, p. 460.
3. *Exodus*, Ch. 20.
4. Orwell, George, "Why I Write," in *CEJL*, Vol. 1, p. 6.

Chapter One

1. Orwell, George. *CEJL*, Vol. 3, p. 394, 406. Also, "You and the Atom Bomb," Vol. 4, p. 6-10. For later articles, see index of Vol. 4.
2. Orwell, George. *Coming Up for Air*. New York and London: Harcourt Brace Jovanovich (A Harvest/HBJ Book), n.d. (first published 1939).
3. Heilbroner, Robert. "Does Capitalism Have a Future?" *New York Times Magazine* (August 15, 1982).
4. Orwell, George. *Nineteen Eighty-Four*. New York: Harcourt, Brace & Co., 1949, p. 208. Hereinafter cited as "Orwell, *1984*..."

Chapter Three

1. Lewis, C. S. "George Orwell," in *Time and Tide* (January 8, 1955). Reprinted in Lewis's *On Stories*.
2. *Ibid.*
3. Orwell, *1984*, p. 1.
4. *Ibid.*, p. 300.
5. *Ibid.*, p. 5.
6. *Ibid.*, p. 99.
7. *Ibid.*, p. 47.
8. *Ibid.*, p. 179.
9. *Ibid.*, p. 87-93.
10. Barron, Neil. Personal communication.
11. Orwell, *1984*, p. 92.
12. *Ibid.*, p. 93.
13. *Ibid.*, p. 5.
14. *Ibid.*, p. 101.

15. *Ibid.*, p. 162.
16. *Ibid.*
17. *Ibid.*
18. *Ibid.*, p. 163.
19. *Ibid.*, p. 164.
20. *Ibid.*
21. *Ibid.*, p. 160.
22. *Ibid.*, p. 161.
23. *Ibid.*
24. *Ibid.*
25. *Ibid.*, p. 177.
26. *CEJL*, Vol. 3, p. 122.
27. *Op. cit.*, p.103.
28. *Ibid.*

CHAPTER FOUR

1. Orwell, *1984*, p. 76.
2. *Ibid.*, p. 56.
3. *Ibid.*, p. 191.
4. Orwell, George. "Charles Dickens," in *CEJL*, Vol. 1, p. 441.
5. Orwell, *1984*, p. 191.
6. Orwell discussed Hopkins's poem in "The Meaning of a Poem," in *CEJL*, Vol. 2, p. 131-134.
7. Licht, Fred. *Goya: The Origins of the Modern Temper in Art*. New York: Universe Books, 1979, p. 253.
8. *Ibid.*, p.269.
9. *Ibid.*

CHAPTER FIVE

1. Orwell, *1984*, p. 3.
2. *Ibid.*, p. 94.
3. *Ibid.*, p. 8.
4. *Ibid.*, p. 94-95.
5. *Ibid.*, p. 112.
6. *Ibid.*, p. 95.
7. *Ibid.*, p. 146-47.
8. *Ibid.*, p. 148.
9. *Ibid.*, p. 152.
10. *Ibid.*, p. 161.
11. Carrington, Robert L. "Rosebud, Dead or Alive: Narrative and Symbolic Structure in *Citizen Kane*," in *Publications of the Modern Language Association* 91 (1976): 185-193.
12. Orwell, *1984*, p. 101.
13. *Ibid.*, p. 224.
14. *Ibid.*, p. 138.
15. *Ibid.*, p. 146-47.
16. Morley, Christopher. *Kitty Foyle*. Philadelphia: J. B. Lippincott Co., 1939.
17. Field, Rachel. *All This and Heaven Too*. New York: Macmillan Co., 1940, p. 139.

18. *Ibid.*, p. 451.
19. *Cold Storage*, in *Five Plays*, by Ronald Ribman. New York: Avon, 1976.
20. Reich, Tova. "Gertrude Stein," in *Harper's Magazine* (August, 1982): 52.
21. Orwell, *1984*, p. 148.
22. *Ibid.*, p. 224.
23. *Ibid.*
24. *Ibid.*, p. 225.
25. Orwell, George. *Keep the Aspidistra Flying*. Harmondsworth, Middlesex, England: Penguin Books, 1962.
26. Alldritt, Keith. *The Making of George Orwell*. New York: St. Martin's Press, 1969, p. 169-172.
27. Crick, Bernard. *George Orwell: A Life*. London: Secker and Warburg, 1980, p. 198.

CHAPTER SIX

1. Dostoevsky, Fyodor. *The Notebooks for the Brothers Karamazov*, edited by Edward Wasiolek. Chicago: Chicago University Press, 1971.
2. Heterotopia, eutopia, and dystopia are all terms constructed from Greek roots, and modeled on the imaginary country Utopia invented by Sir Thomas More for his philosophical fiction of that name, published in 1516. Utopia, which literally means "no place," is the traditional term for a tale presenting a more or less ideal commonwealth. A heterotopia literally indicates an imaginary different place (good or bad). A eutopia is specifically about a good place; and a dystopia presents a bad place—what has been called an "illfare state."
3. Alldritt, Keith. *The Making of George Orwell*. New York: St. Martin's Press, 1969, p. 151.
4. Published in *Tribune* of 12 July 1940, and reprinted in *CEJL*, Vol. 2, No. 11.
5. *Ibid.*, p. 30.
6. *Ibid.*, p. 31.
7. Schiller's Grand Inquisitor was presumably concerned with the salvation of their souls. Did he also care about their happiness? His appearance in the play is perhaps too brief to say.
8. Trilling, Lionel. "Orwell on the Future," in *The New Yorker* (June 8, 1949). Quoted from *Twentieth Century Interpretations of Nineteen Eighty-Four*, edited by Samuel Hynes. Englewood Cliffs, NJ: Prentice-Hall, 1971, p. 25.
9. *CEJL*, Vol. 2, p. 15.
10. Alldritt, *Op. cit.*, p. 15.
11. Quoted from a blurb to an edition of *Nineteen Eighty-Four*.
12. Brown, E. J. *Brave New World, Nineteen Eighty-Four and We: An Essay on Anti-Utopia*. Ann Arbor, MI: Ardis Publishers, 1976, p. 45.

CHAPTER SEVEN

1. Orwell, *1984*, p. 247.
2. *Ibid.*, p. 12.
3. *Ibid.*, p. 18.
4. *Ibid.*, p. 171.

5. *Ibid.*, p. 173.
6. Orwell, George. *Homage to Catalonia.* NY: Beacon Press, 1952, p. 3-4.
7. "Looking Back on the Spanish War." *CEJL*, Vol. 2, p. 264.
8. *Ibid.*, p. 266.
9. *Ibid.*, p. 266-267.
10. Orwell, *1984*, p. 12.
11. *Homage to Catalonia, Ibid.*
12. *CEJL*, Vol. 2, *Ibid.*
13. Orwell, George. *Down and Out in Paris and London.* Garden City, NY: Permabooks, 1954, p. 163.
14. Orwell, George. *The Road to Wigan Pier.* New York: Harcourt Brace & World, 1958, p. 23.
15. *Ibid.*, p. 22.

CHAPTER EIGHT

1. *CEJL*, Vol. 3., p. 210.
2. Orwell, George. *Animal Farm.* New York: Harcourt Brace and Co., 1946, p. 112.
3. Orwell, *1984*, p. 6.
4. *Ibid.*
5. Shakespeare, William. *Macbeth*, Act 1, Scene 1.
6. *Ibid.*
7. Orwell, *1984*, p. 221.
8. *Ibid.*
9. *Ibid.*
10. Orwell, George. "Lear, Tolstoy and the Fool," in *CEJL*, Vol. 4, p. 284.
11. *CEJL*, Vol. 1, p. 6.
12. Island Trees Board of Education vs. Pico, quoted from *Civil Liberties* #343 (July, 1982).
13. Orwell, *1984*, p. 167.
14. *Ibid.*, p. 168.
15. *Ibid.*, p. 303.
16. "The Parking," in *New York Times* (January 3, 1982): 20EY.
17. *CEJL*, Vol. 2, p. 8.
18. *CEJL*, Vol. 3, p. 86.
19. *CEJL*, Vol. 2, p. 7.
20. *CEJL*, Vol. 3, p. 86.
21. Sahz, Prhantas K. Personal communication.
22. Orwell, George. *Homage to Catalonia.* New York: Beacon Press, 1952, p. 40.
23. Crick, p. 245.
24. *CEJL*, Vol. 4, p. 502.
25. Fransl, Albert Bloch. "Die Sprache," in *Epigramme* (Vienna & Leipzig, Verlag, "Die Fackel," 1927, p. 96); quoted from *Karl Kraus*, by Harry Zorn. New York: Twayne Publishers (TWAS 116), 1971, p. 58.
26. Orwell, *1984*, p. 215-16.
27. Crick, p. 3.
28. *Ibid.*
29. *Op. cit*, p. 4.
30. Gary, Leslie. "Rebecca West," in *New York Times Magazine* (April 4, 1982).

CHAPTER NINE

1. Orwell, *1984*, p. 289.
2. First published in Paris in 1899, the book ran through many editions. I used the edition of 1927, designated as 22nd printing. An American translation was published in 1948.
3. Freud, Sigmund. "Notes upon a Case of Obsessional Neurosis," in *The Standard Edition of the Psychological Works of Sigmund Freud*, Vol. 10. London: The Hogarth Press, 1955. The paper was originally published in 1909.
4. Shengold, Leonard. "More about Rats and Rat People," in *International Journal for Psycho-Analysis* 52 (1971), 277-288. This is one of the very few psychological studies that deal explicitly (if, as in this case, only as a sideline) with *Nineteen Eighty-Four*.
5. Orwell, *1984*, p. 145.
6. *Ibid.*, p. 146.
7. *Ibid.*, p. 11.
8. *Ibid.*, p. 16.
9. *Ibid.*, p. 32.
10. *Ibid.*, p. 101.
11. *Ibid.*, p. 128.
12. *Ibid.*, p. 222.
13. Shengold, Leonard. "The Effect of Overstimulation: Rat People," in *International Journal for Psycho-Analysis* 48 (1967), 403-415.

CHAPTER TEN

1. Ibsen wrote *John Gabriel Borkman* in 1896. There are many different English translations available, and it would be useless, therefore, to cite specific scenes or page numbers. This passage is from Act III, Borkman explaining himself to Mrs. Borkman.
2. *Op. cit.*, Act IV., Borkman explaining himself to Ella Rentheim.
3. Mann, Thomas. "Mario and the Magician," in *Death in Venice and Seven Other Stories*. New York: Vintage Books, Random House, 1958, p. 180.
4. *Ibid.*, p. 181.
5. Orwell, *1984*, p. 27.
6. Crick, p. 192.
7. Mann, Thomas. *Joseph the Provider*. New York: Alfred A. Knopf, 1944, p. 417.
8. *Ibid.*
9. Lorenz, Konrad. *On Aggression*. New York: Harcourt Brace & World, 1966, *passim*.
10. Canetti, Elias. *Crowds and Power*. New York: Viking Press, 1966, p. 443.
11. Orwell, *1984*, p. 271.
12. Orwell, George. "Charles Dickens." *CEJL*, Vol. 1, p. 428.
13. Orwell, George. *CEJL*, Vol. 1, p. 336.
14. Rees, Richard. *George Orwell, Fugitive from the Camp of Victory*. Carbondale, IL: Southern Illinois University Press, 1962, p. 64.
15. Howe, Irving, ed. *Nineteen Eighty-Four: Text, Sources, Criticism*. New York: Harcourt, Brace, & World, 1963, p. 202.

16. Orwell, George. *CEJL*, Vol. 1, p. 337.
17. *Ibid.*, Vol. 71, p. 360.
18. *Ibid.*, Vol. 1, p. 377.
19. *Ibid.*, Vol. 4, p. 342.
20. Crick, p. 26.
21. *Ibid.*
22. Orwell, *1984*, p. 269.
23. Mann, "Mario and the Magician," p. 143.
24. Small, Christopher. *The Road to Miniluv: George Orwell, the State, and God*. London: Victor Gollancz, 1975, p. 19.
25. Canetti, p. 295.

CHAPTER ELEVEN

1. Orwell, *1984*, p. 209.
2. *Ibid.*, p. 75-78.
3. *Ibid.*, p. 66.
4. *Ibid.*, p. 69.
5. *Ibid.*, p. 60.
6. Freud, Sigmund. "Medusa's Head," in *Collected Papers*. London: Hogarth Press, 1957, Vol. 5 (written in 1922, first published in *Imago* in 1940).

BIBLIOGRAPHY

A. Books by George Orwell

Animal Farm: A Fairy Story. London: Secker & Warburg, 1945, 91 p.
Burmese Days: A Novel. New York: Harper & Bros., 1934, 371 p.
A Clergyman's Daughter. London: Victor Gollancz, 1935, 317 p.
Collected Essays. London: Secker & Warburg, 1961, 434 p.
The Collected Essays, Journalism, and Letters of George Orwell. London: Secker & Warburg, 1968, 4 vols.
Coming Up for Air. London: Victor Gollancz, 1939, 285 p.
Critical Essays. London: Secker & Warburg, 1946, 169 p. Published in the U.S. as: *Dickens, Dali, and Others: Studies in Popular Culture*.
Down and Out in Paris and London. London: Victor Gollancz, 1933, 288 p.
England, Your England, and Other Essays. London: Secker & Warburg, 1953, 224 p.
The English People. London: Collins, 1947, 47 p.
Homage to Catalonia. London: Secker & Warburg, 1938, 313 p.
Inside the Whale, and Other Essays. London: Victor Gollancz, 1940, 188 p.
James Burnham and The Managerial Review. London: Socialist Book Centre, 1946, 19 p.
Keep the Aspidistra Flying. London: Victor Gollancz, 1936, 318 p.
The Lion and the Unicorn: Socialism and the English Genius. London: Secker & Warburg, 1941, 126 p.
Nineteen Eighty-Four: A Novel. London: Secker & Warburg, 1949, 312 p.
The Road to Wigan Pier. London: Victor Gollancz, 1937, 264 p.
Shooting an Elephant, and Other Essays. London: Secker & Warburg, 1950, 212 p.

B. Selected Critical Monographs

Alldritt, Kenneth. *The Making of George Orwell: An Essay in Literary History*. New York: St. Martin's Press, 1969, 181 p.
Brown, E. J. *Brave New World, Nineteen Eighty-Four, and We: An Essay on Anti-Utopia*. Ann Arbor, MI: Ardis, 1976, 61 p.
Crick, Bernard. *George Orwell: A Life*. London: Secker & Warburg, 1980, xxx+473 p.
Howe, Irving. *Nineteen Eighty-Four: Text, Sources, Criticism*. New York: Harcourt, Brace & World, 1963, 274 p. Expanded as: *Orwell's 1984: Text, Sources, Criticism*. New York: Harcourt Brace Jovanovich, 1982, x+450 p.
Hynes, Samuel, ed. *Twentieth Century Interpretations of Nineteen Eighty-Four: A Collection of Critical Essays*. Englewood Cliffs, NJ: Prentice-Hall, 1971, 117 p.

Meyers, Jeffrey. *George Orwell: An Annotated Bibliography of Criticism*. New York: Garland Publishing, 1977, ix+132 p.
Rees, Richard. *George Orwell, Fugitive from the Camp of Victory*. Carbondale, IL: Southern Illinois University Press, 1962, 151 p.
Small, Christopher. *The Road to Miniluv: George Orwell, the State, and God*. London: Victor Gollancz, 1975, 220 p.

INDEX

Printed in the United States
34555LVS00005B/51

9 780893 704131